Design
FOR
Policy
Sciences

Policy Sciences Book Series

A Series of Studies, Textbooks, and Reference Works

Edited by YEHEZKEL DROR

Hebrew University of Jerusalem

PUBLISHED

Yehezkel Dror
Design for Policy Sciences, 1971

Yehezkel Dror
Ventures in Policy Sciences, 1971

Harold D. Lasswell
A Pre-View of Policy Sciences, 1971

Beatrice K. Rome and Sydney C. Rome
Organizational Growth through Decisionmaking, 1971

Walter Williams
Social Policy Research and Analysis, 1971

IN PREPARATION

Benson D. Adams
Ballistic Missile Defense

Joseph P. Martino
Technological Forecasting for Decisionmaking

Design
FOR
Policy
Sciences

YEHEZKEL DROR

The Hebrew University of Jerusalem
The World Institute, Jerusalem, Israel

American Elsevier
Publishing Company, Inc.
NEW YORK

AMERICAN ELSEVIER PUBLISHING COMPANY, INC.
52 Vanderbilt Avenue, New York, N.Y. 10017

ELSEVIER PUBLISHING COMPANY, LTD.
Barking, Essex, England

ELSEVIER PUBLISHING COMPANY
335 Jan Van Galenstraat, P.O. Box 211
Amsterdam, The Netherlands

International Standard Book Number 0-444-00105-0

Library of Congress Card Number 74-158631

Manufactured in the United States of America

TO MY MOTHER

Stephanie Friemann (Altman)

Contents

Preface

This short volume is devoted to the presentation of the idea of policy sciences, as a new supradiscipline based on novel scientific paradigms. My main thesis is that contemporary scientific approaches are inadequate for meeting the requirements of relevance and the needs of humanity. Urgently required, therefore, is a different scientific approach, orientation, methodology, and method—which I call, following Harold D. Lasswell, "policy sciences."

Policy sciences is concerned with the contributions of systematic knowledge, structured rationality and organized creativity to better policymaking. It constitutes a main effort to reassert the role of intellectualism and rationalism in guiding human destiny. Without impairing the importance of other society shaping forces, such as moral prophecy and mass movements, I claim that policy sciences is essential for improvement of the human condition, and, indeed, for avoidance of catastrophe.

Going beyond the domain of academia, the emergence of policy sciences constitutes a scientific revolution, which involves radical changes in accepted patterns of research, teaching, and academic professionalism; even more important and difficult, policy sciences involves fargoing changes in politics. Such implications are closely tied in with the nature of policy sciences and its base characteristics. Therefore, in this book I explore the main implications of policy sciences for academia and for politics, in addition to presenting the case for policy sciences, exploring its main paradigms, and examining some of its main dimensions.

This book is directed at the growing community of persons worried about the relations between knowledge and power and about the social significance and the social uses of science. In particular, I hope the main ideas of this book may be of interest to scholars, scientists, and students, and to various policy professions—such as planners, systems analysts, environmental engineers, defense analysts, public health experts, lawyers, public commentators, and so on. Hopefully, politicians, senior government and corporate executives, and a growing number of "enlightened citizens" may also wish to confront the issues posed in this volume.

The limited ambition of this book is to present the idea of policy sciences and some of its implications. In order to sharpen the message and serve the mission, this book is concise and radical. Issues are presented in sharp colors without doing justice to all the variety and heterogeneity of reality. Also, this book fails to reflect adequately the doubts and misgivings that should and do accompany so new and untested an endeavor as the proposed development of policy sciences. I do recognize the inadequacy of the descriptions, evaluations, and prescriptions presented in this book; but I think the inadequacies relate to details and not to the main thesis. By directly putting forth the case for policy sciences, I hope to focus the judgment of the reader on main issues, rather than to dissipate his concern among minutiae.

Readers interested in pursuing at greater depth, and with more details and operationalization, some basic theories and focal concepts of policy sciences are referred to my earlier book, *Public Policymaking Reexamined* (San Francisco: Chandler Publishing Co., 1968), and to my companion volume, *Ventures in Policy Sciences* (New York: American Elsevier, 1971). *Public Policymaking Reexamined* provides a general theory of policymaking as a basis for policy sciences. *Ventures in Policy Sciences* includes an integrated set of essays which analyze various policy sciences concepts and apply them to concrete issues in different countries.

This book is the result of personal contemplation. But its final version owes much to stimulation provided by my colleagues and friends at The Rand Corporation, where I was privileged to spend nearly two and a half years, on leave from the Hebrew University of Jerusalem. I am also indebted to a number of programs in policy sciences at universities in the United States, with which I had the privilege to be associated, and to many individuals—both academicians and policy professionals—who helped me to develop my thinking. But despite my intellectual and personal debt to many persons and institutions, this book is a private creation of mine, for which only I myself am responsible.

YEHEZKEL DROR

Jerusalem, Israel

PART I

The Inadequacy
of Contemporary Sciences

The development of policy sciences is a serious and difficult endeavor, which needs justification. Intellectual curiosity and the challenges of a new scientific endeavor may be reason enough for some scholars to devote themselves to policy sciences. But more is needed to prove the case.

It is the inability of contemporary sciences to meet urgent policymaking needs which makes policy sciences so essential. This inadequacy of contemporary sciences is examined in Part I. At first, I discuss some weaknesses shared by contributions to policy by all contemporary sciences. Then, I explore two clusters of disciplines which should be particularly relevant for better policymaking, namely, behaviorial sciences and management sciences. Finally, the special needs of accelerated modernization policies are used as a test for policy contributions by science. The overall conclusion of Part I is that policy sciences is urgently required, because contemporary sciences cannot provide sufficient help—neither now nor in the future—in significantly improving policymaking.

CHAPTER 1

Common Weaknesses of Science Contributions to Policy

To judge by the number of scientists presenting policy recommendations in public, or signing petitions, or advocating one or another solution to some fashionable issue, contemporary science has much to contribute to policy-making. But when we penetrate beyond the noise screen and subject the recommendations that presume to be based on science to careful examination, we are often surprised and even shocked. It is indeed amazing how scientists who are most careful about their specific area of research and who rigorously check every finding for reliability and validity make very elementary mistakes when entering the domain of policy.

Many (though certainly not all) policy recommendations presented by scientists, and presuming to rely on science, suffer from a number of serious weaknesses, including in particular, the following:

1. A tendency to formulate problems narrowly, to fit into a specialized perception set. Thus, an economist tends to view all problems as economic ones; an engineer, as technological ones; and a depth psychologist, as dominated by personality dynamics.

2. Not only are problems perceived through narrow "tunnel vision," but the theories (tacit and even explicit) used to analyze the problems are taken from specialized disciplines, with little attention to borders of validity. Thus, life scientists tend toward biological models of all phenomena; the single-minded image of policy issues held my many engineers is clearly related to mechanical models; and economists fondly claim universal applicability for their sophisticated resources allocation and optimization models, while implicitly often still holding on to the "economic man."

3. In respect to proposals for solutions, scientists tend toward one of two extremes: either they stay within their narrow perspectives and propose as solutions policy instruments belonging to their specific disciplines, or they freely propose (and with an air of self-assurance) activities going far beyond their areas of competence. It is hard to decide which one of these two evils is worse—the civil engineer proposing new housing technologies as a cure for urban problems or the physical scientist proposing a complex arms limitation treaty. My own feeling is that the narrow specialist who uses his scientific credentials to propose comprehensive policies is more dangerous, because the weaknesses of his position are often not obvious; but narrow proposals for complex issues are also often useless and sometimes dangerous.

3

A mismatch between the domain of validity of a discipline and the space of a policy issue is the underlying cause of the three above-mentioned weaknesses of many policy recommendations presented by scientists in the name of their expertise. These weaknesses can be summed up as narrow, mono-disciplinary perspectives, which produce single-dimensional images of multispace issues; a distorted perception of problems; careless transgressions beyond one's area of scientific competence; and zero-effective, if not counter-productive, recommendations.

More fundamental, more difficult to treat, and, to a large degree, a cause of such mismatch, are the absence of prescriptive methodology in most disciplines and the lack of knowledge by most scientists of even rudimentary elements of policy prescriptive approaches.

To clarify this point, let me distinguish between three levels of scientific knowledge, as viewed from the standpoint of human action: knowledge permitting control and direction of the environment; knowledge permitting control and direction of society and individuals; and knowledge regarding the directory of the environment, society, and individual-controlling and -directing activities, that is, regarding *meta-direction* and *metacontrol*.

Scientific knowledge of the control and direction of the environment, as supplied by rapid progress in the physical sciences, is the most highly developed level. Scientific knowledge of the control and direction of society and individuals is much less advanced, but at least the behavorial disciplines constitute recognized components of science, receive significant support, and do show some signs of progress. Least developed of all and scarcely recognized as a distinct focus for research and study are meta-direction and metacontrol knowledge.

The absence of meta-direction and metacontrol knowledge not only constitutes a serious lacuna in scientific inputs into policymaking, but also hinders transformation of available scientific knowledge into policy recommendations, because policy recommendations must be based on some fusion between prescriptive methodologists and knowledge of the environment, society, and individuals. The absence of such methodology results in some fundamental weaknesses of many presumedly science-based policy recommendations. These weakness include the following in particular:

4. A mix-up between reliable factual knowledge, implicit axiomatic assumptions, provisional theories, conceptual taxonomies, doubtful hypotheses, and various types of hidden value judgments, such as on substantial goals, on willingness to take risks, and on evaluation of time.

5. The neglect of important special characteristics and requirements of policy-oriented research, such as time scarcity, the search for leverage points, the need for social invention, and the necessity for social experimentation.

6. The neglect of the dominant characteristics of politics and policymaking and of the relations between substantial policy issues and the characteristics of policymaking. As a result, we get oscillation between naivety and cynicism and, therefore, between disregard for implementation problems and Machiavellian tactics. Also, as a result, little attention is devoted to improvements of the policymaking system itself (with some exceptions in political science, most of them quite traditional) as a main avenue for better resolutions of social problems.

7. Often, a tendency to ignore resources limitations and therefore to avoid the necessity of evaluating alternatives within a benefit-cost-risk framework.

8. The absence of criteria for evaluating the significance of issues and, therefore, a strong susceptibility to issue fashions, disproportionalism, and even sensationalism.

Scientists are now caught in a dilemma. On one hand, there are student pressures for relevance, feelings of guilt, a sense of moral obligation to help, and perhaps some hidden urge for power. But these motives are met, on the other hand, by the policy sterility of contemporary scientific knowledge and the policy-irrelevant structure of contemporary scientific institutions. There is something pathetic about the modes in which many scientists try to overcome this dilemma and search for ways to gear themselves to policy issues. It is not for lack of good intentions and intense efforts that these attempts usually (though not always) result in dismal failure, more often hindering good policymaking than advancing it. But—because of the absence of self-sophistication and nonexistence of qualified "peers" equipped to judge the quality of contributions to policymaking—the scientific community tends to be unaware of the weaknesses of its contributions to policymaking. Instead, scientists tend to blame politics and politicians for stubbornly refusing to follow the light provided by whatever and whoever are regarded as the relevant sciences and their accepted spokesmen (which change, sometimes as the result of fashions, as illustrated by the rapid acceptance of ecological sciences).

Upon reflection, one should be little surprised by the inability of physical sciences to be of significant help in policymaking. After all, their world is radically different from the world of social behavior and policy phenomena. Therefore, it is enough if physical sciences provide us with the foundations of new technologies to be used as policy instruments, without playing a major role in decisionmaking on the preferable utilization of these instruments. If we add that physical sciences can provide an excellent training of the mind and thus do produce a few brilliant policy analysts who, on their own, succeed in making the radical transition from the world of physics to society and policy—this is more than enough. The only requirement must be that physical scientists recognize the limitations of their disciplinal relevance for policymaking. The same applies to large parts of life sciences and to many branches of pure mathematics (but not theory of games, for instance). These disciplines provide basic knowledge and lay the foundations for advancing policy-instrument-providing technology. Thus they fulfill an essential social function, and there is no justification to require of these disciplines additional policy contributions.

The situation is radically different in two other clusters of science, namely, the behavorial (or social) sciences and the management (and decision) sciences. Explicitly oriented toward understanding society, the behavorial sciences can be expected to serve as a solid basis for better policymaking. And explicitly oriented toward the improvement of management and decisionmaking, management sciences presume to be directly applicable for policymaking improvement. Because of their apparent relevance to policymaking and the great promise they seem to hold forth, a more detailed examination of the policy significance of behavorial sciences and of management sciences is required.

CHAPTER 2

Particular Weaknesses of Behavioral Sciences

The search for help from behavorial sciences for policymaking is an intensive one, which has been going on for quite a long time. It well antecedes modern behavorial sciences, as illustrated, for instance, by the work of Jeremy Bentham in England and by the Cameralists in Europe. The founders of modern sociology were strongly interested in policy implications of their knowledge, some of them trying to combine knowledge and power through personal political activity—as illustrated, for instance, by Max Weber himself. In more recent periods, the question "Knowledge for what?" has been asked continuously in the behavioral sciences community, and efforts to apply behavorial sciences to social issues have been made for many years. Even when measured by quantitative criteria, the investments in behavioral sciences research in the United States, including so-called applied studies, are considerable.

Despite such intense interest in applied behavorial sciences, including significant work in Europe, the output of behavioral sciences in terms of explicit policy-relevant knowledge is hard to pin down. There exists significant knowledge relevent to some problems. But a behavorial scientist who is asked to demonstrate the possible operational significance of his disciplines for the main policy issues facing humanity and society is quite hard put to provide illustrations. One can go through one behavioral sciences book after another without being able to identify more than a handful of policy-relevant items. This is the case also when we adopt (as we should) a broad concept of "policy-relevant knowledge," which looks for heuristic aids and not for answers. Even when we accept as relevant, knowledge that mainly serves to educate the frames of appreciation of policymakers in policy-salient ways, not many behavioral sciences theories and items will pass this minimal threshold.

A good illustration is provided by the report of the Special Commission on the Social Sciences of the National Science Board, *Knowledge into Action: Improving the Nation's Use of the Social Sciences* (1969). The Commission clearly tried hard to prove the importance of the behavioral sciences for social problems and action. Nevertheless, the report is not at all convincing to someone who is not convinced in advance. This is an exact reflection of reality and not of any lack of effort on the part of the Commission.

Not only are contemporary behavioral sciences disappointing in policy

7

relevance, but no promising ways to change this situation through incremental adjustments are discernible. Suggestions for incremental change vary from doing more of what is being done now, to setting up additional problem-oriented social research organizations. Some of the proposals are highly interesting and promise to be useful, such as those of the Behavioral and Social Sciences Survey Committee of the United States National Academy of Sciences, *The Behavioral and Social Sciences: Outlook and Need* (Englewood Cliffs, N.J.: Prentice-Hall, 1969). But most of the suggestions do not face the main requisites of the quantum jumps in scientific approaches necessary for developing significant policy-relevant behavorial sciences inputs.

The issues and problems of applied behavioral sciences are not easy to discuss. This is the case because of the heterogeneous composition of applied behavioral sciences and the complexity of relations between pure behavioral science and applied behavorial science.

The widespread use of the term *applied behavioral science* in the singular may be misleading in its connotation that there is some unitary referent to this verbal symbol. What we do have are a number of behavioral sciences, which in different forms are or can be applied to a large range of policy issues. The main relevant behavioral sciences include, in particular, sociology, social psychology, and political sciences.

A special case not usually included in the term *behavioral sciences* is economics, which has unique characteristics, including much fusion of pure and applied elements. Well-recognized reasons for the special nature of economics include the different intellectual history of economics, which has been more policy-oriented; the susceptibility of large parts of its subject matter to quantitative treatment; the reductionability of many of its variables to a limited number of main aggregate categories which are operational and measurable; and the relatively simple characteristics of some main category interrelations, which permit quite isomorphic simulation of important aspects of economic phenomena in modern societies by compact and exercisable models (especially simultaneous equations and, nowadays, computer programs).

Highly significant is an additional characteristic of economics which played a special role in its successes as advanced policy-relevant knowledge, namely, the fusion in economics between behavioral sciences knowledge and a prescriptive methodology. Economics covers two main types of concerns: knowledge about economic institutions and behavior and ways to direct them, and knowledge of how to "economize," in the sense of optimizing utilization of scarce resources. It seems to me that this fusion in economics is a main source of its strength as policy-relevant knowledge, serving in this respect as a pioneer for policy sciences. At the same time, one should recognize that large parts of economics are weak in their behavioral contents. As a result, when actual behavior does not fit implicit behavioral assumptions, then contemporary economic theory provides wrong recommendations. This is the case for instance, in respect to both modernization countries (i.e., technologically underdeveloped countries) and a growing number of situations in what I call "saturated societies."

However one explains the special situation of economics and whether or not one accepts my view of it as a leading case on fusion between prescriptive methodology and behavioral sciences knowledge, economics clearly is in a separate category. Therefore, I am excluding it from the following treatment of behavioral sciences, focusing my concerns on sociology, social psychology, and political science.

To generalize from the heterogeneous bundle of application attempts belonging to sociology, social psychology, and political science, it is clear that many attempts have suffered and, to a lesser degree, still suffer from well-recognized weaknesses. These weaknesses include, in particular (*a*) oscillation between idiographic micro-studies and "grand theory"; (*b*) a priori commitment to equilibrium and structural-function concepts, which result in do-nothing, or, at best, incremental-change recommendations; (*c*) timidness in facing acute social issues and in handling taboo subjects; (*d*) perfectionism, which causes withdrawal from problems with time constraints, that is, all significant policy issues; and (*e*) a deep feeling of guilt about getting involved in applications which go beyond "value-free," "pure," "factual," and "behavioral" research.

As just mentioned, these weaknesses are well recognized by a growing number of behavioral scientists, who are increasingly committed to contributing their knowledge to the improvement of the human and societal condition. These behavioral scientists are supported by growing demands by government and a variety of clients and publics for behavioral sciences help in facing policy issues, by student pressure for relevance, and by a number of foundations and research centers. The first fruits of a new type of applied behavioral sciences can be detected in ideas such as social reporting and social indicators; in policy-oriented methodologies, such as evaluative research and social experimentation; in attempts to frankly face value issues; in orientations toward the future dimension; in broader approaches to social policy issues; in adoption of advocacy roles; and, most important of all, in reputedly substantive inputs into a few important decisions and recommendations, such as in the United States the antisegregation Supreme Court decisions and the report of the Commission on Violence, as well as specific inputs into many current decision processes. Also significant is the increasing amount of work dealing with policymaking as a subject for research and improvement and with the role of scientists in policymaking.

This list of achievements looks impressive. And, indeed, it reflects significant progress in applied behavioral sciences. But, in order to get a more balanced view, a number of other points must be taken into account:

1. In many cases where behavioral sciences inputs are reputed to influence decisions, they may serve as supportive briefs for decisions actually arrived at independent of the behavioral sciences inputs.

2. The advances in applied behavioral sciences do not constitute an integrated and mutually reinforced set of activities. Instead, different items are developed in mutual isolation. As an illustration, most work on substantive issues ignores the studies on policymaking and their implication for political feasibility and for institutional requisites of changing present policies. Similarly, most studies on substantive issues ignore work on relevant alternative futures and neglect the necessity to adjust recommendations in light of longer-range perspectives. At the same time, studies on policymaking are seldom related to policy issues and also pay little attention to relevant alternative futures; and studies of alternative futures tend to neglect the future dimensions both of policymaking and of main policy issues.

3. Applied behavioral sciences still occupy a marginal position in their disciplines. Only fractions, even though increasing ones, of research time are allocated to them. More significant is the marginal position of applied work in respect to recognition; thus, it seems that applied subjects are not acceptable as doctorate thesis subjects at the large majority of graduate behavioral sciences departments.

4. Applied behavioral sciences are just now moving from unself-consciousness to self-consciousness, in the sense of developing a self-identity and building up their own frames of appreciation, methodology, and institutions. Different behavioral sciences still tend to have their own applied corners, with significant differences, for instance, between applied political science and applied sociology. As a result, the need to reorganize the behavioral sciences system as a whole for application is only slowly gaining recognition. Even such an obvious need as adjusting graduate teaching to prepare behavioral sciences professionals for policy-relevant roles is only slowly being recognized and even more slowly being acted upon. Also widely ignored are problems such as the organizational location of behavioral sciences advisors, required interaction arrangements between them and senior policymakers to enable the latter to utilize behavioral sciences, the novel roles of policy research organizations, and so on.

5. These weaknesses in self-perception of applied behavioral sciences are well demonstrated, for instance, by the widespread tendency to compare applied behavioral sciences and their relation to pure behavioral sciences with engineering and its relations to physical sciences. This comparison ignores such basic differences as the following:

a. The pragmatic base of much engineering, which anteceded physical science knowledge and in some areas still operates quite well on a pragmatic basis (e.g., acoustics and metallurgy), versus the impossibility of basing applied behavioral sciences on similar pragmatic sources of invention and knowledge. (In this respect, politicians and executives are more in accord with pragmatic periods and areas of engineering.)

b. The existence in engineering of a clear chain from abstract knowledge to production, moving from pure research through development, engineering, and pilot-testing to production, versus the completely different nature and unstructured relationship between pure and applied behavioral sciences.

c. The inherent differences between physical sciences knowledge and behavioral sciences knowledge.

d. The differences between engineering a "product," in the sense of a tangible, material thing, and dealing with societal issues, which are in part intangible, immaterial, undefined, open, dynamic, contextually shaped, and value-dominated.

e. The scarcity of pure behavioral sciences knowledge on which application can be based and, therefore, the fallacy of comparison with the engineering phase, which takes the existence of relevant pure knowledge and its continuing progress more or less for granted, or at least as something not to be planned for as an integral part of engineering. The situation is different in behavioral sciences, where encouragement of application-relevant abstract research may be a main requirement for useful applications.

Most serious of all the symptoms and consequences of the unself-consciousness of applied behavioral sciences is the already mentioned absence of a methodology for prescriptive and policy-oriented behavioral sciences endeavors.

Let me emphasize that I am speaking about the absence of a methodology for prescriptive and policy-oriented study. Certainly, behavioral sciences are not lacking an analytic basis for their traditional main areas of concern— descriptions, analysis, and understanding of behavior. But the needs of prescriptive and policy-oriented research are quite different and require methodologies of their own. The absence of such methodologies is one of the main reasons for the inadequacy of most contemporary behavioral sciences for the improvement of policymaking.

CHAPTER 3

Particular Weaknesses of Management Sciences

If a main weakness of behavioral sciences is the absence of a prescriptive methdology, then—so the uninformed may say—the answers should be provided by the disciplines which specialize in prescriptive methodology, namely, the management sciences (including micro-economics). Indeed, the most important and, in some respects, the most promising effort to provide scientific aid for managing complex systems and improving decisionmaking is going on within management sciences. But upon closer examination the management sciences too must be appraised as unable to meet the needs of improved policymaking.

It is not easy to discuss management sciences as a whole because quite a heterogeneous set of orientations, perceptions, methodologies, techniques, and tools are at one time or another covered by that term. Therefore, every discussion of management sciences can easily be contradicted by the statement that the disputant has in mind quite a different concept of management sciences. Also, because many leading management scientists are brilliant persons, it is not difficult to quote a view of authors to contradict every critic.

Because of this vagueness of the concept "management sciences," let me antecede discussion of their inadequacies with a few observations on what I am talking about. I am not discussing expressions of good intentions or exhortations of what management sciences should be or prophecies of what management sciences may be like in the undefined future. My subject is management sciences as they are now and as they can be expected to be, unless they change radically.

Management sciences can in part be circumscribed by enumeration of some disciplines that overlap with them, include them, or constitute elements of them. The more relevant ones include operations research (sometimes called "operational research"), decision sciences, management cybernetics, information theory, managerial economics, parts of organization theory, systems engineering, engineering economics, and systems analysis. For convenience, I will refer in this paper to all these disciplines and research areas as management sciences.

All management sciences share a number of philosophic assumptions, especially on the role of rationality, the significance of human decisionmaking, and a number of theories, especially utility theory and micro-economics. They also share (*a*) a basic frame of appreciation, namely "system ap-

12

proach," and (*b*) a series of tools, namely "quantitative techniques."

Most present uses of management sciences are conditioned more by the quantitative techniques than by the systems approach. The quantitative techniques include, in the main, linear and dynamic programing, queueing theory, Markov chains, network analysis, game theory, simulation (in part with the help of the other tools), benefit-cost analysis, and decision analysis. Recently, less rigorous tools have also been developed in order to handle some situations, for instance, gaming (which has a long history in the military) and Delphi Method.

For policymaking purposes, the systems approach is more important than the quantitative tools. Basically, the systems approach recognizes that different problems, issues, and events are closely interrelated. Therefore, it is impossible to know whether improvement of any single component will help achievement of the overall system goals, without examination of the impacts of any particular change on the operations of the system as a whole. In practice (and even in theory) it is of course impossible to examine all system effects for all times. But the systems approach at least recognizes the problem and proposes some improvements of practice, by enlarging the scope of consequences to be appraised when evaluating different alternatives. When we face a confined problem, such as replacement decisions, we can often mathematically simulate all of the relevant system and thus arrive at an *optimal solution* for the relevant system as a whole. When we face more complex issues, such as transportation, we can at least be sensitized to the need to appraise impacts, for instance, on leisure time, population dispersal, shopping habits, community structure, etc. Also, by taking a broader systems view, we can often reformulate the decision problem in a way permitting better solutions. Thus, instead of asking ourselves how to improve peak-hour transportation, we may reformulate the question to how to reduce peak-hour traffic demand—which may bring up for consideration completely different alternatives (e.g., staggering work hours, changing physical planning to have people live nearer their place of work, or encouraging shopping by mail or through wired television). Thus, while in respect to a complex system we cannot hope to arrive at an optimal solution, we often can, with the help of the systems approach, identify a *preferable solution* (i.e., a solution demonstrably better than those otherwise arrived at, but falling short of the usual requirements of optimality).

Essential for application of the systems approach to any concrete problem is the availability of some methodology for predicting (at least in probabilistic terms) the impacts of different alternatives on overall operations of the relevant system. The various quantitative techniques of management sciences serve mainly to fulfill this need; they constitute models of the relevant system, permitting the prediction of system impacts through trying out the various alternatives on the model instead of on reality. Till very recently, such models have usually been quantitative, taking the form of equations or computer programs. This has imposed strict limitations on the domain of applicability of the systems approach, which was bound by dependence on the availability of quantitative data and models. Progress in computer technology holds forth the promise of very powerful programs which may be able to handle highly complex relationships between large numbers of variables, and which therefore can simulate more complicated systems. Even more important for the handling of complex policy issues is the increasing recognition that the systems approach can be of much help, even in the absence of quantitative simulation techniques, by providing improved qualitative insights and permitting the development and utilization of decision-improving methodologies other than quantitative techniques.

Encouraged by the obvious potentials of management sciences and by significant successes in some areas, many management scientists naturally want to move on from the very limited issues with which they have been dealing to the more comprehensive societal problems to which contemporary society gets increasingly sensitized. But for purposes of better policymaking, management sciences tend to be inadequate in a number of important respects:

1. Management sciences try to propose optimal policies while neglecting the institutional contexts of both the problems and the policymaking and policy-implementation processes. Thus, "institution building" is not within their domain.

2. Management sciences are unable to handle political needs, such as consensus maintenance and coalition building.

3. Management sciences are unable to deal with irrational phenomena, such as ideologies, charisma, high-risk commitments, self-sacrifice, and unconventional styles of life.

4. Management sciences are unable to deal with basic value issues and often inadequately explicate the value assumptions of analysis.

5. Management sciences deal with identifying optimal alternatives among available or easily synthesized ones. The invention of basically new alternatives is beyond their scope, though they can sometimes help by showing the inadequacy of all available alternatives.

6. Management sciences require some predictability in respect to alternatives. Situations of "primary uncertainty" (when not only the probabilities of various outcomes but the dimensions of the possible outcomes are unknown) cannot be handled by them.

7. Management sciences depend on significant quantification of main relevant variables and the availability of models permitting "exercising" of

these variables. Therefore, complex social issues cannot be dealt with and most behavioral sciences knowledge is ignored.

8. Basic choices on what I call "megapolicies" (see pages 63–73), such as attitudes to risk and time, are not explicitly faced by management sciences. Rather, maximin or minimax and discount of the future ("positive interest rates") are usually assumed.

9. Management sciences neglect the metapolicy level (the level of policies on how to make policy) nearly completely. Improvement of the policy-making system is beyond the scope of management sciences, even though critical for the improvement of policymaking.

These nine characteristics are not equally shared by all management sciences studies. Some of the main pioneers of management sciences clearly label such characteristics as inadequate and diligently search for ways to overcome them. But, if we look on available management sciences studies of real issues rather than at professions of faith, introductory statements, or single outstanding studies, then this list of inadequacies of present management sciences may justly be criticized as overmild.

Let me try to illustrate weaknesses of contemporary management sciences by the enumeration of some typical (though not universal) omissions in three areas of studies:

a. *Transportation studies:* Preoccupation with "mix-of-modes" issues and with satisfaction of extrapolated consumer demands, within a benefit-cost frame. Some attention to pollution effects, especially when susceptible to translation into economic values. Ignorance of changes in the values to be served by future transportation, such as transportation tastes, aesthetic feelings, new patterns of leisure time use. Neglect of transportation impacts on community life and social interaction. Ignorance of possible positive functions of inadequate transportation. Ignorance of political and power implications of transportation. Inadequate treatment of interfaces between transportation and communication, housing, and various aspects of the patterning of human activities in space.

b. *Defense studies:* Preoccupation with low-level aspects of defense, including equipment and tactics. Inability to face issues of non-rational adversaries. Little explication of basic value assumptions and of scenarios based on radically different assumptions. Ignorance of internal political and cultural conditions and domestic implications of external defense policies. Very weak treatment of interfaces between socio-political-cultural issues and defense issues in other countries. Very weak treatment of relations between defense activities and other external activities, especially socio-economic ones.

  c. Public safety studies: Tendency to define public safety in symptomatic rather than fundamental terms, that is, number of crimes, rather than feeling of safety or propensity to deviate. Concentration on efficiency of law enforcement, rather than underlying causes of problems. Short-range approach, with very little attention to longer-range interfaces between public safety and, for instance, youth culture.

The necessity to extend the boundaries of management sciences so as to permit their utilization for handling complex issues is closely related to the desire to improve policymaking. When main policies can be taken for granted and when spontaneous adjustment of policies to changing needs through incremental change can be relied upon, then main concern with the improvement of managerial decisions is justified. But when the main policies themselves are in need of formulation or reformulation, then improvement of managerial decisions, which aim at implementation of existing policies, is not only useless, but often counter-productive. The dangers here are double: (*a*) diverting attention and other scarce improvement resources from primary issues to secondary issues; and, even more serious, (*b*) doing more efficiently the incorrect thing, and therefore both causing damage more effectively and making the wrong policy more difficult to change. Better logistics for wrong wars, improved programing for projects which should not be undertaken at all, and sophisticated gravity analysis for urban services location when the basic structure of the city and of the services should be changed—these are some illustrations of improving, through management sciences, decisions which implement a policy which first should be reformulated.

My conclusion is that management sciences provide approaches and tools useful for the improvement of some types of management decisions and even some subpolicies. But management sciences are unable to contribute much to better policymaking. Furthermore, their very contribution to managerial decisions makes better policymaking all the more urgent during periods of rapid change, such as the present epoch. This requirement cannot be met by the management sciences themselves.

CHAPTER 4

The Case of Accelerated Modernization Policies

The inadequacies of contemporary sciences are clearly brought out when we examine their actual and potential contributions to the improvement of accelerated modernization policies. This is an important test, both (*a*) because accelerated modernization policies are important for the majority of mankind, and (*b*) because accelerated modernization policies are representative in many respects of a broader category, namely, change policies under conditions of rapid social transformation.

Efforts to direct change under conditions of rapid social transformation (which, in turn, may be accentuated because of the direction efforts) constitute a main challenge facing policymaking at present and in the foreseeable future. Whether we look at modernization societies; at saturated societies, such as the United States; at post-ideological states, such as the Soviet Union; at societal subunits, such as urban concentrations and youth groups; or at intersocietal groups, such as various European supranational bodies or the United Nations, a main policy challenge is shared by all: the desire and perceived necessity to direct, or at least influence and control, ongoing transformations, including both their rate and their directions.

In many respects, the issues of policymaking on the direction of rapid social transformations are more difficult in the modern countries. Certainly, from the point of view of human destiny, the risks resulting from bad policymaking in the modern countries are at present greater than those resulting from bad policymaking in the modernization countries, because of the impact of modern countries on modernization countries and the possibly global consequences of radical breakdowns in the highly industrialized, technological, and science-intense countries, which can easily reach dimensions of catastrophe for the human species as a whole. But it is easier to analyze problems located somewhere else. Therefore, and because more relevant experience is available, I will try to bring out the weaknesses of contemporary sciences in respect to policymaking on the direction of rapid social transformations by examining the particular case of accelerated modernization policies. Most of the findings on the inadequacies of contemporary sciences in respect to accelerated modernization policies apply even more so to social-transformation-directing policies in the various types of modern countries, though some findings must be adjusted.

To start with some details, I will examine the potential contributions of

17

behavioral sciences and of management sciences to the improvement of accelerated modernization policies, by policy issue areas and by main policy-making phases, including metapolicymaking. The most convenient way to present this examination is in the form of four tables. (See tables 1, 2, 3. and 4.)

Unavoidably, the findings presented in the four tables are too concise, overgeneralized, and somewhat dogmatic in form. But I do think their overall *Gestalt* is correct and does reflect both the limited utility and the strong inadequacy of contemporary behavioral sciences and of contemporary management sciences as contributors to improved policymaking for accelerated modernization.

Problems of accelerated modernization provide quite a shock to contemporary sciences, which were and still are mainly based on Western experience and mainly directed at expressing and meeting Western values and Western conditions. This applies to basic models, such as the equilibrium and balance models of behavioral sciences; this applies to underlying values and assumptions, such as the fixation of economies on Gross National Product and its assumptions on infrastructure; this applies to implicitly accepted feasibility images, such as maintenance standards of engineering; this applies to admission criteria of professions, such as the requirements for licensing to practice medicine; and this applies to modes of problem selection, such as the concern of management sciences with low-level managerial issues.

There has been some increased sensitization to the need to adjust contemporary sciences for the problems of accelerated modernization, as illustrated by new subdisciplines, such as comparative administration, development economics, and area studies. Recently these efforts, at least in part, have slowed down—perhaps because of a new sense of trouble in the modern countries themselves. In any case, contemporary sciences remain inadequate, and present developments in modern countries may lead to even less concern with accelerated-modernization-relevant issues. A good illustration is the pollution issue, which receives rapidly increasing attention by contemporary scientists (most of whom are concentrated in the West), while definitely being of minor concern in the foreseeable future for modernization countries, which are suffering from much more acute problems.

I want to avoid overexaggeration. Contemporary sciences can contribute much to modernization issues if suitable subjects are studied, and there is some progress in this direction. But well supported is the overall conclusion that contemporary sciences are inadequate for the improvement of accelerated modernization policymaking. By analogue, this finding also indicates that contemporary sciences are inadequate for urgently needed better policy-making on the direction of rapid social transformation in the modern countries.

Table 1

Possible Contributions of Behavioral Sciences to
Improvement of Accelerated Modernization Policies, by Policy Issue Area

Problem Area	Behavioral Sciences Useless	Behavioral Sciences Helpful	Behavioral Sciences Very Helpful
Agriculture	Degrees of innovation: R&D; land use and product mix	Land reform; aggregate resources allocation; internal political implications; degrees of diversification; main development directions; foreign implications; land reallocation; monitoring system; irrigation, distribution, and marketing systems	Attitudes toward work; training
Culture	Metaphysical, social, and political values	"National Identity"; encouragement of indigenous art and creative crafts; attitudes toward rationality; language; ethnic problems; clash between traditional and modernizing values; some aspects of written language development; mass communication; communication network construction and management	
Defense	Main goals; aggregate resources commitment; strategies and basic postures; estimation of protection needs; weapon systems choices; specific resource allocation; force composition; defense RD&E; defense production; low-level weapon mix	Basic internal political implications; internal problems of army politics; external aid and procurement opportunities; logistics, communication, and some manpower problems	

Table 1 (*continued*)

Problem Area	Behavioral Sciences Useless	Behavioral Sciences Helpful	Behavioral Sciences Very Helpful
Education and Manpower	Aggregate resource allocation; propensities to innovate; integration with basic economic, social, and foreign policies; educational networks; curriculum programming; facility planning	Main strategies (cadre training, mass education, technological education, etc.); political and ideological implications; learning methods and devices; "brain drain"; location of facilities; teaching-manpower utilization; some manpower planning, facility programming and utilization	Teacher training
Foreign Relations	Main goals; resource commitment; basic strategies and involvements; country investment benefit cost estimation	Internal political implications; prediction of exogenous variables; some aspects of external presentation network (e.g., location, communication, logistics)	
Health	Aggregate resource commitment; main strategies; medical R&D	Basic structure (public insurance, etc.); recruitment and handling of foreign aid; concepts of health; political and professional aspects (e.g., feasibility of using non-professional practitioners); some aspects of treatment systems; some aspects of training of professionals; facility planning; facility programming and utilization	Problems of "health nature," health habits, and healing traditions

Table 1 (*continued*)

Problem Area	Behavioral Sciences Useless	Behavioral Sciences Helpful	Behavioral Science Very Helpful
Industrialization	Main strategies; risk policy; resource commitment; basic instruments (public initiative, encouragement of private enterprise, etc.); project choice; R&D policy; sector interdependence	External aid recruitment and handling; monitoring system; marketing planning, project planning, and implementation	Attitudes toward work
Internal Politics	Leader recruitment and development; political cohesion; elite transformation; propensities to innovate; political ideologies and values; rules of succession	"Nation-building" strategies; coalition building and maintenance; conflict management; transfer of power to modernizing agents; ethnic problems, etc.; communication and political socialization networks; some problems of internal security; some technical issues, such as election organization	
Population	Demographic strategy; resource commitment	Ideological, cultural, and political feasibility; external implications and pressures; comparison of alternative control methods; information and propaganda system; incentive system; monitoring system; distribution network for control devices and their logistics	

Table 2

Possible Contributions of Behavioral Sciences to
Improvement of Accelerated Modernization Policies, by Policymaking Phases

Elements of Preferable Policymaking	Some Implications of Possible Uses of Behavioral Sciences
a. Basic goal clarification	Analysis of behavioral compatibility of different values; prediction of social conditions of various values and of their social consequences; some information on value changes processes; Some clarification of conditions of consensus and agreement on basic goals
	No direct or heuristic application to goal determination and ordering
	Dangerous in providing simplified value assumptions (e.g., "economic man") and overgeneralizing from normal behavior
b. Megapolicy clarification	Supply of knowledge of actual megapolicy tendencies, such as incrementalism, risk repression, short-range time perspectives, and satisficing
	No direct or heuristic application to megapolicy determination and ordering
	Dangerous in supplying recommendations and models which often are inappropriate ,such as preferences for balanced development, comprehensive planning, and incremental change
c. Issue formulation	Some aid in "lookout" and estimation of social significance of issues
d. Alternative identification	Supply of knowledge about variables influencing propensity to innovate. Some comparative data that can stimulate alternative innovation
	No direct aid for invention of novel alternatives
e. (1) Consequence prediction	Some knowledge useful for prediction of social consequences of some alternatives in specific policy areas
(2) Identification of preferable alternative	Of no help, other than as indicated in e (1)
f. Approval and implementation considerations	Some knowledge of political, organizational, and social feasibility. This permits some prediction of feasibility and some indication of institutional and other changes required for increasing feasibility
g. Feedback and policy reformulation	Some knowledge about organizational and individual barriers to feedback and policy reformulation, such as tendency for postdecisional dissonance reduction, political-organizational-psychological "sunk costs," and goal-succession difficulties. This knowledge is useful for designing preferable feedback networks

Table 2 (*continued*)

Elements of Preferable Policymaking	Some Implications of Possible Uses of Behavioral Sciences
Policymaking system improvemnet	Some knowledge of features of actual policymaking systems and their dynamics. Some specific suggestions for minor improvements
	Of no help for novadesigning policymaking systems and of little help for significantly redesigning policymaking systems. Dangerous, in overemphasizing change difficulties and risks of innovation

Note: The phases are based on Yehezkel Dror, *Public Policymaking Reexamined* (San Francisco: Chandler Publishing Co., 1968), pp. 163 ff, and "Uses of Systems Approach and Quantitative Techniques in Policy Formation," in United Nations, *Use of Modern Management Techniques in the Public Administration of Developing Countries* (forthcoming).

Table 3

Possible Contributions of Management Sciences Techniques to Improvement of Accelerated Modernization Policies by Policy Issue Area

Problem Area	Quantitative Techniques Useless	Quantitative Technique Helpful	Quantitative Technique Very Helpful
Agriculture	Land reform; aggregate resources commitment; internal political implications; degrees of innovation; degrees of diversification; main development directions; foreign implications; attitudes toward work	R&D; land reallocation; training; monitoring system	Land use and product mix; irrigation, distribution, and marketing systems
Culture	"National Identity"; encouragement of indigenous art and creative crafts; attitudes toward rationality; metaphysical, social, and political values; language; ethnic problems; clash between traditional and modernizing values	Some aspects of written language development; mass communication	Communication network construction and management
Defense	Main goals; aggregate resources commitment; basic internal political implications; strategies and basic postures; internal problems of army politics; external aid and procurement opportunities	Estimation of protection needs; weapon systems choices; specific resource allocation; force composition; defense RD&E; defense production	Low-level weapon mix; logistics, communication, and some manpower problems
Education and Manpower	Main strategies (cadre training, mass education, technological education, etc.); political and ideological implications; aggregate resource allocation; teacher training; propensities to innovate; integration with basic economic, social, and foreign policies	Learning methods and devices; "brain drain"; educational networks; location of facilities; teaching-manpower utilization; curriculum programing; some manpower planning; facility planning	Facility programming and utilization

Table 3 (*continued*)

Problem Area	Quantitative Techniques Useless	Quantitative Technique Helpful	Quantitative Technique Very Helpful
Foreign Relations	Main goals; resources commitment; internal political implications; basic strategies and involvements	Prediction of exogenous variables; country investment benefit-cost estimation	Some aspects of external presentation network (e.g., location, communication, logistics)
Health	Aggregate resource commitment; main strategies; basic structure (public insurance, etc.); problems of "health culture," health habits, and healing traditions; recruitment and handling of foreign aid; concepts of health; political and professional aspects (e.g., feasibility of using nonprofessional practitioners)	Some aspects of treatment systems; some aspects of training of professionals; medical R&D; facility planning	Facility programming and implementation
Industrialization	Main strategies; risk policy; resource commitment; basic instruments (public initiative, encouragement of private enterprise, etc.); external aid recruitment and handling; attitudes toward work	Project choice; R&D policy; monitoring system; sector interdependence; marketing planning	Project programming and implementation
Internal Politics	"Nation-building" strategies; coalition building and maintenance; leader recruitment and development; political cohesion; elite transformation; propensities to innovate; political ideologies and values; rules of succession; conflict management; transfer of power to modernizing agents; ethnic problems, etc.	Communication and political socialization networks; some problems of internal security	Some technical issues, such as election organization
Population	Demographic strategy; ideological, cultural, and political feasibility; resource commitment; external implications and pressures	Comparison of alternative control methods; information and propaganda system; incentive system; monitoring system	Distribution network for control devices and their logistics

Table 4

Possible Contributions of Management Sciences Techniques
Improvement of Accelerated Modernization Policies, by Policymaking Phases

Elements of Preferable Policymaking	Some Indications of Possible Uses of Quantitative Techniques
a. Basic goal clarification	Supply of some heuristically useful concepts, such as "utility," exchange rates, welfare function, opportunity costs, etc. Provision of some optimization concepts, such as Pareto Optimality. Advanced areas, such as coalition theory and collective decision theory, help to clarify conditions of consensus and agreement on basic goals
	No direct and strict applications to goal determination and ordering
	Dangerous in presenting "reasonable" assumptions which, nevertheless, may not apply (such as transitivity of preferences) and in hiding value assumptions behind some criteria (e.g., Pareto Optimality ignores dogmatic and compact ideologies or situations where making someone else suffer is a main objective)
b. Megapolicy clarification	Supply of many heuristically useful concepts, especially from theory of games, such as mixed and pure strategies; minimax; maximin and maximax; lottery value; and principle of minimum regret. Some ideas for handling time, such as "interest rates," and some principles for handling uncertainty.
	No direct and strict applications to megapolicy determination and ordering
	Dangerous in supplying concepts which often are inapplicable and can be easily misleading, such as "interest rates"
c. Issue formulation	Possible supply of some helpful frames of references but nothing of direct applicability
	Dangerous if formulation is influenced by desire to make issue treatable by quantitative tools
d. Alternative identification	Nearly useless for identification of new alternatives which cannot be synthesized from available ones
	Very dangerous in emphasizing choice limited to available alternatives and in having a bias toward alternatives with which there is some experience (concerning which data permitting uses of quantitative techniques is available)
e. (1) Consequence prediction	Supply of important methods for predictions, such as simulation, extrapolation, and Delphi. Supply of important concepts for dealing with uncertainty, such as "subjective probability" and Bayesian calculus. Supply of important tools for absorbing uncertainty, such as sensitivity testing and hedging

Table 4 (*continued*)

Elements of Preferable Policymaking	Some Indications of Possible Uses of Quantitative Techniques
	Dangerous in tending to cover objective uncertainty with facades (such as subjective uncertainty) and in tending to accept implicitly maximin and incremental change megapolicies.
(2) Identification of preferable alternative	Supply of a basic conceptual framework, namely, benefit-cost. Supply of additional important concepts, such as criteria for decision criteria. Also often some parts of expected consequences can be reduced to forms permitting direct application of quantitative techniques, such as calculation of expected net benefit
	Dangerous because of trend to emphasize those consequences which can be handled quantitatively and, therefore, to neglect other consequences which cannot be handled quantitatively and which sometimes cannot even be satisfactorily conceptualized
f. Approval and implementation considerations	Supply of some useful concepts and heuristic aids, such as the idea of network analysis, which can be applied to alternative approval and implementation arrangement
	Dangerous in encouraging very misleading analogues, such as between political power and economic capital or technological production capacity
g. Feedback and policy reformulation	Supply of some useful concepts, such as "feedback" and its related phenomena. Supply of some techniques directly applicable to some aspects of feedback structuring (such as dynamic sampling) and some frameworks in part applicable to some feedback problems (such as PERT)
	Dangerous when leading to concentration of feedback on those features only which can be handled quantitatively
Policymaking system improvement	Supply of some methodologies and techniques which constitute useful policymaking improvements, such as aspects of PPBS and the quantitative techniques themselves. Provision of some concepts and frameworks heuristically useful for analysis of the policymaking system and indicating some improvement directions, for instance, through cybernetic models of the policymaking system. But most aspects of the policymaking system and most improvement directions are beyond quantitative techniques
	Limited danger, because the inapplicability of quantitative techniques to policy-making system improvement is so obvious as to restrain illusions and misuse

Note: The phases are based on Yehezkel Dror, *Public Policymaking Reexamined* (San Francisco: Chandler Publishing Co., 1968), pp. 163 ff, and "Uses of Systems Approach and Quantitative Techniques in Policy Formation", in United Nations, *Use of Modern Management Techniques in the Public Administration of Developing Countries* (forthcoming).

CHAPTER 5

Conclusion: The Need for a Scientific Revolution

The inescapable conclusion from our examination is that contemporary sciences are inadequate for improving policymaking. This inadequacy is not the result of underdevelopment of one discipline or another; rather, this inadequacy is built into the very characteristics of contemporary sciences. Therefore, if we want significantly to increase the contributions of science to better policymaking, a new scientific approach is needed. Using the terminology of Thomas S. Kuhn,[1] our conclusion can be formulated as follows: The inadequacy of present normal sciences for the purposes of policymaking improvement is the result of their basic paradigms. Therefore, in order to produce the scientific inputs necessary for policymaking improvement, a scientific revolution is essential.

This does not imply that the new paradigms should displace those of contemporary sciences. Contemporary sciences are well equipped to fulfill important functions other than policymaking improvement, such as increasing human comprehension of the universe, satisfying human curiosity, providing intellectual challenge, and supplying very useful technologies. Furthermore, contemporary sciences also have important contributions to make to better policymaking, by providing knowledge on policy subject matters and supplying policy instruments.

Therefore, findings on the necessity of new paradigms for a new policy sciences are not a substitute for the need to accelerate progress of parts of contemporary sciences. For better policymaking, both the establishment of policy sciences and the advancement of some parts of contemporary sciences are essential. Furthermore, there two requirements are mutually interdependent. In the absence of policy sciences, it is not clear what inputs from contemporary sciences are necessary for improved policymaking and how they may be used. With policy sciences, a synergetic relationship can be established: contemporary sciences will provide basic knowledge on which policy sciences will be, in part, based; policy sciences will stimulate parts of contemporary

[1]See Thomas S. Kuhn, *The Structure of Scientific Revolutions* (Chicago: University of Chicago Press, 1962).

For a critical discussion of this concept in respect to social sciences, see Robert W. Friedrichs, *A Sociology of Sociology* (New York: Free Press, 1970), in particular chapters 1 and 2.

sciences for more policymaking-relevant activities and will improve the utilization of inputs of contemporary sciences in actual policymaking; and contemporary sciences will produce more knowledge on policy instruments and on policy issues, relevant for improved policymaking.

For the improvement of policymaking with the help of science, both the advancement of parts of contemporary sciences and the establishment of policy sciences are needed. But those are not enough. Better contributions by science to improved policymaking depend not only on the existence of suitable scientific knowledge. Also essential are changes within the policy-making system and in the connecting links between the policymaking system and the scientific system, so as to permit and encourage integration of scientific knowledge into actual policymaking.[2]

Improving the contributions of science to better policymaking (including necessary changes in the science system, in the policymaking system, and in their interconnections) is, in turn, only one of a much broader series of changes needed for better policymaking. Better political leadership, innovations in the moral sense of the population, social prophecy, democratic personalities—these are illustrations of other requisites of significantly improved policymaking. Some of these changes can be induced with the help of scientific inputs into policymaking, some depend on social movements which are beyond contemporary understanding and control, and some appear to our present limited mind as quasi-random phenomena (or as supernatural interventions). But all of them are factors strongly influencing the qualities of policymaking.

This book is mainly concerned with one of the requirements of better policymaking, namely, the design of a new scientific approach. However, I realize that this is only one of the needs of better policymaking, though an absolutely essential one, which should provide help also in meeting some of the other requirements as I shall try to show later.

Approaches
to Policy Sciences

The urgent need for policy sciences seems quite obvious. The next questions, therefore, are why policy sciences is so slow in coming and what progress in the direction of policy sciences, if any, has taken place.

Part II addresses these two questions. In chapter 6, some of the barriers to policy sciences are explored, including barriers within the science community, barriers within the policymaking community, and barriers in society at large. These barriers are very strong and explain the tardiness of policy sciences. Nevertheless, some beginnings of policy sciences can be discerned. These beginnings are surveyed in chapter 7, with special attention to the short histories of strategic analysis and futures studies, both of which provide a number of lessons for policy sciences.

CHAPTER 6

Barriers to Policy Sciences

The need for changes in science in order to increase relevance to policymaking has been recognized often. The question "Knowledge for what?" has been asked and forgotten many times over, with little impact on scientific activity and, till very recently, hardly a movement in the direction of policy sciences.

In a society as plagued by difficult policy issues and as strongly committed to the ideology of science (and, till recently, as intensely believing in science) as modern Western culture, the slowness of progress in developing a scientific approach geared to the needs of policymaking must be caused by powerful barriers. The fact that a sophisticated version of policy sciences was proposed by Harold D. Lasswell twenty years ago[1] and was widely discussed but not taken up precludes lack of invention as an explanation for the slowness of acceptance and development of such an approach. Other barriers must be at work.

A careful study of the barriers to policy sciences (which overlap in part with the broader set of barriers to policy-relevant knowledge as a whole, including also barriers to policy-oriented work in contemporary sciences) is not only interesting but essential for overcoming them. Such a study is itself an appropriate subject matter for policy sciences. Even in the absence of specific studies dealing with this matter, available experience and knowledge permit the presentation of at least some hypotheses on causes for the slow progress of the policy sciences idea up till now. Some of the causes are endemic to the science community, others to the policymaking community, while still others belong to culture and society as a whole.

The strong resistance of the science community to changes in the basic paradigms of science and in the disciplinary structure of scientific activity is by now a well-recognized phenomenon. The more right I am in my findings on the inadequacies of contemporary sciences for better policymaking and the necessity, therefore, for a new scientific approach based on novel paradigms and involving novel structures, the more science's conservatism constitutes a barrier to the development of policy sciences. When we present the new paradigms of policy sciences, the differences between them and contemporary sciences will become clear, thus explaining why resistance to changes in the foundations of science must operate as a very strong barrier to policy

[1] In Daniel Lerner and Harold D. Lasswell, eds., *The Policy Sciences: Recent Developments in Scope and Methods* (Stanford: Stanford University Press, 1951).

33

sciences. It is beyond the scope of this work to examine the multiple factors causing such resistance to change in the scientific community, factors which include *inter alia* the ideology of science, the social institutions of science, and the organizational characteristics of research and teaching units. But I want to concretize one especially relevant set of barriers to policy sciences operating in the scientific community by exploring the distances between applied behavioral sciences and management sciences.

This is a good illustration, because the necessity to achieve some fusion, or at least interface, between applied behavioral sciences and management sciences is a minimum requirement, not only for policy sciences, but of much less ambitious efforts for teamwork on policy problems. The need for such teamwork is well recognized and many attempts have been made to satisfy it, but it seems that such attempts usually fail. Even in policy research organizations, which explicitly devote themselves to policy research and deny loyalty to the traditional divisions of knowledge, the degree of interdisciplinary work is disappointingly low. There seem to be too many differences between applied behavioral sciences and management sciences to permit cooperation, not to speak of integration.

These differences seem to include the following:

	Management Sciences	Applied Behavioral Sciences
a. Differences in disciplinary bases	Economics, engineering, mathematics, operations research, decision sciences	Behavioral sciences
b. Differences in main areas of application	Defense, water resources, hardware systems, transportation, some urban management	Social subproblems related to welfare, communities, individuals
c. Differences in basic methodology	Prescriptive, rational, cost-benefit	Behavioral research methods
d. Differences in value orientations	"Efficiency," with increasing interest in "equity"	"Good life," "social justice," "humanism," "social integration," "minority rights"
e. Differences in professional codes	Special relations with employer, often "the establishment"	Ideology of "free profession," though dependent on academic institutions, foundations, and contracting organizations

	Management Sciences	Applied Behavioral Sciences
f. Differences in reference groups	Mixed between peer orientation and much orientation toward policymakers	Much peer orientation; some orientation to action groups
g. Differences in success expectation	Low	Oscillating between optimism and pessimism
h. Differences in modes of work	Teamwork, moving from problem to problem	Individual work and some teamwork; often specialization in particular problems
i. Differences in organizational loci	Mainly small groups in regular organizations; some special policy research organizations, both profit and independent nonprofit corporations	Mainly university departments and university institutes; some nonprofit organizations
j. Differences in career patterns	Continuous career and specific professional commitment; some exchange with teaching	Part of academic discipline; limited commitment to applied work, often auxiliary to teaching and academic research
k. Differences of culture	More clinical, detached, objectivizing, externalizing, analytical	More personally committed, emotional, attached to subjects of study
l. Differences in political opinions (in the United States)	More conservative, "law and order"	More radical, "anti-establishment"
m. Differences in personality patterns	There seem to be significant differences in personality patterns. Their specifications must wait for suitable research.	

Based on personal observation and impressions rather than on a systematic survey, this list of differences is unreliable in its items. But I think it is valid in pointing out the overall *Gestalt* differences between management sciences and applied behavioral sciences. Thus, it can serve to illustrate one type of barrier to policy sciences in the science community, namely, the barriers, to interdisciplinary endeavors. There are many other types of barriers, as already indicated. But this one is an especially important barrier to policy sciences, which must be overcome as a precondition for any progress.

When we go on to the policymaking community, the barriers to policy sciences look even more forbidding, though they are less direct. These barriers cannot really stop policy sciences from developing within the scientific community, though they can retard its development and minimize its utilization for the improvement of actual policymaking.

To understand the strength of the barriers to policy sciences within the policymaking community, it is necessary to realize that policy sciences aspires to penetrate into the innermost process of policymaking and decisionmaking, which, up till now, have been regarded as the exclusive domain of policymakers and decisionmakers. In distinction from contemporary sciences, policy sciences does not limit itself to providing data which the policymaker is assumed to take into account. Neither does policy sciences express itself in clear-cut recommendations for the policymakers to follow, as are proposed today by many scientists—who thus behave in a way which at least is easily comprehensible to policymakers and familiar to them from the operation of interest groups and lobbying groups. Policy sciences aspires to do something different, namely, to tell the policymakers how to make decisions, how to structure themselves for better policymaking, and how to train themselves for better policymaking.

In chapter 16, some implications of policy sciences for politics will be examined, and we will see that the main functions allocated to politics by democratic ideology will not only not be impaired by policy sciences, but rather will be enhanced and aided by it. At the same time, policy sciences does involve fargoing changes in many features of policymaking, including its political components. It is the apprehension of those changes which constitutes a main basis for the resistance to policy sciences in the policymaking community. Indeed, when the implications of policy sciences are better, but not yet fully, understood, more active hostility to policy sciences by second-class politicians and executives must be expected, because the less competent ones will rightly feel their positions endangered by the progress of policy sciences.

On a more operational level, quite a number of barriers in the policymaking community to policy sciences can be identified, which in part result from the just-discussed feeling of apprehension, in part reflect soon to be discussed social prototypes and expectations, and in part reflect diffuse resistance to change. Barriers to policy sciences in the policymaking community can already be observed in action, even though policy sciences is only in *status nascendi*. The best expression of these barriers in operation is behavior toward independent policy research organizations, and policy research in general. This behavior ranges from active hostility, legal restriction on research and on foundation support, and budgetary stringency, to wide-spread lack of support, noncooperation, and cold-shouldering of research results.

I do not claim that these behavior patterns are universal. They are not. Barriers to policy sciences collide with the obvious needs of policymakers for whatever help they can get and the persisting prestige of science in contemporary society. Therefore, many instances of encouragement of policy research organizations and of policy research components of the policymaking system do occur. Furthermore, in a number of countries, efforts are made to establish policy-sciences-oriented units within the policymaking system. In the United States, the staff of Dr. Henry Kissinger and the former National Goals Research Staff in the White House serve as interesting illustrations. The Planning Staff in the Office of the Chancellor in the Federal Republic of Germany and some units in the Canadian Privy Council exemplify the beginnings of such activities in other countries.

Examination of these and other units would lead us too far away from the subject of this book. Let me, therefore, limit myself to three comments: (*a*) Much of the support, insofar as it does exist, goes in the direction of specific efforts to improve decisionmaking in particular areas (e.g., foreign affairs) or by specific methods (e.g., PPBS). While useful and sometimes in the right direction, it falls far short of supporting policy sciences and of adopting a positive view of policy sciences research as a whole. (*b*) As yet, even limited support for such specific endeavors enjoys only very narrow and temporary successes, as illustrated by the regress of the PPBS attempts in the United States (*c*) Nearly all such cases depend, for the initiation and continuation, on rather accidental personal interest and personal support by top-level individual policymakers.

Despite some countervailing forces, the barriers to policy sciences in the policymaking community clearly still have the upper hand and will, I think, become stronger before they become weaker. In particular, the following specific barriers can be identified:

1. Lack of belief in the ability of science to be of help in the policymaking process, which is regarded quasi-mystically as an art which is monopolized by the "experienced politician and decisionmaker."

2. Strong taboos and ritualistic attachments to institutions and beliefs which are expected (often, rightly so) to be undermined if or when policy sciences develops.

3. Socio-culture distance between scientists and policymakers, on more complex lines than C. P. Snow's Two Cultures thesis, but nevertheless very pronounced.

4. Incapacity to understand science contributions to policymaking, both

because such contributions tend to be presented in overtechnical form and because most policymakers are underqualified in relevant knowledge. Such lack of understanding generates anxiety and results in either overrejection of science contribution or overacceptance, the latter of which in turn results later on in disappointment and rejection.

5. Bewilderment at the contradictory conclusions arrived at by equally reputable scientists and therefore a tendency to ignore scientific contribution as a whole. This is caused by the mixed-up structure of contemporary science contributions to policymaking, on one hand, and the unsophisticated view of science held by many policymakers, on the other hand.

6. Bad experience with scientists and with science contributions to policymaking, which suffer from all the weaknesses discussed in Part I, and/or adopt a clear partisan stance. Particularly barrier-reinforcing are the political naivety and political ignorance of the large majority of science contributions and their lack of saliency for the policymakers' perspectives.

7. Bad experience with the misuse of scientific jargon and quantitative techniques used to "snowball" policymakers and overwhelm them so as to get them to adopt one conclusion or another. This is tied in to the widespread tendency to use scientific evidence as briefs to support partisan positions arrived at earlier without the benefit of scientific inputs.

8. Discord between the formats of good policy studies and the habits of policymaking. I will elaborate this point in chapter 10. In short, policy sciences sharpens alternatives, poses explicated choices between different values and assumptions, clarifies goals which can then serve as criteria for evaluating the quality of policies, recognizes uncertainties, and makes visible parts of the modes in which decisions are reached. All these features contradict the usual contemporary patterns of policymaking, including those of individuals, groups, and organizations.

9. A correct feeling that the development of policy sciences and the increasing use of policy sciences in policymaking are not technical changes, but involve some shifts in power—both within the traditional components of the policymaking system and from them to new components, including policy scientists and policy sciences research organizations.

More diffuse than the barriers to policy sciences in the policymaking community are the barriers posed by some widespread features of society and culture as a whole. Taboos in respect to many institutions are one of these barriers, though nowadays in many countries a slightly less important one, thanks to the accelerated rate of social transformation. The two main interrelated social-cultural barriers to policy sciences—in the United States and in most other Western countries, seem to be (*a*) fear of the policymaking roles of science and (*b*) same beginnings of an antiintellectual and antirational movement.

The fear that scientists may take over and become a new compact ruling class—in line with a shallow reading of Plato's *Republic*—is a widespread theme in contemplative literature. "Managerial revolution," "technocracy," "meritocracy," "technopolis"—these are some of the forms in which the danger of scientocracy is presented. Never mind that it is a counterfactual fear, as is shown in the Epilogue. The existence of such an apprehension is what counts. Through direct impact on public opinions, through acceptance in the policymaking community, and through being taken seriously even in parts of the science community itself, the "helltopia" of scientocracy constitutes an important barrier to policy sciences.

Apprehension of scientocracy was, until recently, accompanied by the widespread belief that, at least in all other aspects, science is a blessing to mankind. Nowadays, especially in the saturated United States, where the benefits of science can be taken for granted, this belief is changing. Increasingly, science is regarded as a Pandora's box, breeding dangers to humanity, therefore to be controlled and perhaps even restrained. In some groups a more radical antiscience attitude can be discerned, with rejection of intellectualism and rationality as main avenues for human progress, and preference, instead, for mystic and para-scientific experiences. It is not interest in altered states of consciousness as such which constitutes a barrier to policy sciences; altered states of consciousness are a legitimate concern for science and may be a significant subject for policy sciences, as I will mention later on. It is the antiintellectual and antirational context within which much of the psychedelic culture operates which, among much more important dangers for society, makes it a potentially important barrier to policy sciences. This, in particular, poses some problems for policy sciences at universities, where student culture is directly confronted. (I will return to this problem in chapters 13 and 14.)

Many of the barriers to policy sciences interact through positive feedback with the underdevelopment of policy sciences; because of the barriers, policy sciences does not really get started and attempts to develop it have a hard time. The absence of policy sciences in turn reinforces many of the barriers. For instance, doubts in the science community about policy sciences are reinforced by the absence of demonstrations that policy sciences is possible and useful; doubts in the policymaking community about contributions by science are reinforced by the weaknesses of contemporary science inputs, which in turn are largely a result of the absence of policy sciences; and student skepticism about the relevance of science is based on the actual irrelevance of much of contemporary science for critical policy issues, which again is largely a result of the absence of policy sciences.

We have here a magic circle which perpetuates and reinforces itself. What is needed is a break in the positive feedbacks which bar policy sciences. This break must come from policy sciences itself. If policy sciences reaches a critical achievement level, then (*a*) it will be supported by increasing parts of the science community; (*b*) it will be in increasing demand by high-quality components of the policymaking community; and (*c*) it will demonstrate the essential contributions which a new scientific approach can make to human destiny, and thus reassert the role of intellectualism and rationality in human self-direction and mobilize support from groups that are "concerned" and look for relevance.

I do not imply that the way will be easy or that success is assured. Endeavors to build up policy sciences may fail because they are beyond present human capabilities or because they will be stopped by the various barriers before policy sciences achieves a critical mass. Alternatively, societies may be drawn into downward whirlpools much too strong to be reversed by rational action. But the effort is surely worth trying. Indeed, some beginnings of policy sciences are already under way, showing that with devotion and determination it may be possible to overcome the barriers and to achieve a "taking-off" stage.

CHAPTER 7

Some Beginnings and Their Lessons

Despite all the barriers, the needs for policy sciences are increasingly recognized and some efforts to get it started can be identified. In recent years, efforts to establish and advance policy sciences include the following:

1. Reports by various commissions on the uses of knowledge and science, all of which reached the conclusion that some changes are needed in science itself.

Especially revealing are, for instance, the Report by the National Academy of Sciences on *The Behavioral Sciences and the Federal Government* (1968), and the Report of the National Sciences Board, *Knowledge into Action: Improving the Nation's Use of the Social Sciences* (1969).

2. The proliferation of interest by scientists in the social implications of knowledge, accompanied by demands for reorientation of science. This trend is well reflected, for instance, in the *Bulletin of the Atomic Scientists: Science and Public Affairs, The Smithsonian, Science,* and *The American Scientist.*

3. The development of new disciplines and subdisciplines directly concerned with policymaking. Such disciplines and subdisciplines include, for instance, strategic studies and futures studies, which I will soon discuss at greater length. Also relevant are many of the already explored activities going on under the name of "applied social sciences" and within management sciences.

4. The invention and development of new types of policy research organizations which in effect engage in the development and application of policy sciences. The Hudson Institute, the Urban Institute, parts of the Brookings Institution, the new Woodrow Wilson Foundation, the Institute for the Future, The Rand Corporation, and The New York City Rand Institute illustrate this trend in the United States. Similar organizations are being established, *inter alia,* in the Federal Republic of Germany, Israel, Canada, and Japan.

5. The self-development and self-education of outstanding individual policy scientists, who, thanks to their personal multidisciplinary background, accidents of opportunity, and their interest in the application of scientific methods to policy problems, went into the pioneering of policy sciences, thus demonstrating the feasibility of policy sciences and its promises.

6. The recent establishment of new university programs devoted to policy sciences, with or without use of that term. In the United States alone, more than ten such programs were initiated during the last few years. For instance,

between 1968 and 1970, graduate policy sciences programs have been set up in the United States at the following universities: Carnegie-Mellon University, Harvard University, University of California at Berkeley, University of Michigan, University of Pennsylvania, University of Texas, and State University of New York at Buffalo. These programs describe themselves in terms such as *policy sciences, public policy, policy analysis,* and *public affairs,* but, in contents and orientation, all move in the direction of policy sciences.

7. The rapid increase in the number of conferences, books, periodicals, "invisible colleges," and similar expressions of professional activity and interest devoted in effect to the advancement of policy sciences as a whole or of some of its major aspects. To pick some illustrations from recently founded periodicals, *Policy Sciences, Public Policy, Public Choice,* and *Social Policy* directly reflect this interest. Less directly related, but still relevant, are periodicals such as *Futures, Long-Range Planning,* and *Technical Forecasting and Social Change.*

Some of these beginnings, are important as signs of growing interest in policy sciences and as *prima facie* proof that the barriers are not insurmountable and that efforts to advance policy sciences are feasible. These beginnings are also important as providing some learning opportunities on which to base the upbuilding of policy sciences. In later parts of this book, I will refer to various items of experience, such as that of policy research organizations and of policy sciences university programs. At present, I want to explore some implications of two disciplinary precursors of policy sciences, namely, strategic analysis[1] and futures studies.

Strategic analysis and futures studies have both developed mainly during the last ten to fifteen years. They share an interest in policy issues and, at least in part, an orientation toward better policymaking. At the same time, they are also different from one another in many important respects, such as goals, methodologies, underlying disciplines, audience and clientele, organizational locations, personality of the main involved scholars, explicit and tacit values, nearness to policymakers, dependence on "hard data," and more. Despite these differences—and, in part, thanks to them—strategic analysis and futures studies in combination do provide a great many experiences which are important for the future development of policy sciences.

---

[1]When strategic analysis is considered as a precedent for policy sciences, a number of advantages originally held by strategic analysis and absent in policy sciences must be born in mind. These include the following: (1) the subject matter was novel, no experience with nuclear confrontations being available; (2) no academic discipline or group of practitioners could convincingly claim expertise and thus monopolize the subject; (3) the subject was recognized as critical, thus making policymakers eager for help from wherever available; and (4) bipolar confrontation was relatively easy to analyze, permitting striking and convincing findings without advanced methodologies.

The experiences of strategic analysis and future studies which are most salient for the development of policy sciences can be summed up as follows:

1. It is possible to develop policy sciences knowledge. Despite the various barriers discussed in this chapter and the inherent intellectual difficulties facing policy sciences—despite all of them, it is feasible to arrive at understandings, methodologies, and findings which can make significant contributions to policymaking and which constitute essential components of policy sciences. These components are diverse in their contents and characteristics, as illustrated by the differences between the more imaginative aspects of futures studies, on one extreme, and the rigorous quantitative characteristics of some components of strategic analysis, on the other extreme. But, in principle, the job of building up policy sciences is not beyond human capacities—as clearly brought out by advances in strategic analysis and in futures studies.

2. The development of policy sciences knowledge has largely taken place outside the conventional academic structure. While progress in the direction of policy sciences is possible, as demonstrated by futures studies and strategic analysis, much of this progress has taken place outside conventional disciplines and outside traditional university locations. One of the striking features of strategic analysis and, even more so, of futures studies is that their development was pioneered by persons who clearly transgressed beyond the boundaries of their traditional disciplines of origin; furthermore, much—if not most—of the buildup of strategic analysis and of futures studies occurred outside universities—either at special policy research organizations or by individuals working on their own, unattached to the traditional university structure. While parts of strategic analysis gained recognition and did become established within existing or new departments and university institutes, futures studies have continued to grow and develop outside the university structure, building up new networks and new institutions of their own. A difference between strategic analysis and futures studies which should be noted here as again illustrating the diversity of useful policy sciences approaches is the important role of nonacademicians, in the traditional sense of the term, in the development of futures studies. Publicists and journalists have made important contributions to futures studies, while in strategic analysis most of the scholars are members of the academic community, even though they have left their traditional disciplines and moved over to a new area created by themselves.

3. Novel organizational and professional expressions have been developed. The relation of the development of futures studies and strategic analysis to the establishment of new organizational structures has already been indicated, but it is so important as to deserve further emphasis. In particular, the evolution of strategic analysis is very closely related to the establishment of "civilian

strategists" as a new profession, and of special independent policy research organizations as a main location for strategic analysis. The establishment of novel professional roles of civilian strategists and of new types of research organizations in which strategic analysis is located was not only essential for the advancement of strategic analysis itself, but was also essential to achieve the necessary rapport with policymakers—including access for information, for interaction during the analysis, and for presentation of the findings of the analysis. Futures studies have not yet developed unique professional and organizational roles of their own, though some beginnings can be discerned— in the form of forecasting staff in private corporations, special lookout and forecasting organizations, and some international networks for building up futures studies. This very underdevelopment of specific professional and organizational arrangements for futures studies is closely correlated with some of the main weaknesses of futures studies, to be discussed in the next point.

4. There are dangers of overpopularity. Futures studies serve as an important learning opportunity for policy sciences, not only by their achievements, but also—and perhaps even more so—by their failures. Most prominent among the latter is a tendency of futures studies toward sensationalism, fashionalism, and sometimes even some opportunism. In the absence of any institutionalization which serves to screen the reliable from the illusionary and the imaginative from the hallucinatory, everyone who feels he has something to say on the future can label himself as a "futurologist" and present his private images of the future as if they constituted the results of careful study combined with creative imagination. The absence of any external signs permitting discrimination between futures studies that should be taken more seriously and those which had better be completely ignored makes it very hard to utilize futures studies as a serious endeavor which should constitute an important component of policy sciences.[2] The implications for policy sciences as a whole are quite clear: in the absence of some screening mechanisms, the flag of policy sciences may be indiscriminately utilized by incompetent persons and even by charlatans—thus ruining any chance for the development of policy sciences as a scientific and professional endeavor. At the same time, the experience of the better parts of futures studies indicates a necessity to avoid too rigid a screening, which may prevent imaginative work and unconventional creativity from making urgently needed contributions to policy sciences and, via them, to the improvement of policymaking.

5. An impact on policymaking is possible. The experiences of strategic

---

[2]For a series of guidelines on how to build up policy-oriented futures studies, see Yehezkel Dror, *Ventures in Policy Sciences* (New York: American Elsevier, 1971), chapter 5.

analysis and, to a lesser degree, of futures studies illustrate possibilities to achieve actual impact on policymaking. Thus, apprehensions that policy sciences is a vain endeavor because, in any case, policymaking cannot be influenced are, to some extent, refuted by the experience of strategic analysis, and, less so, of futures studies. This does not imply that policy sciences will easily influence policymaking. But the possibility to influence policymaking through intellectual findings—both directly in respect to specific policies, megapolicies, and metapolicies, and indirectly through educational effects and reshaping of the frames of appreciation of policymakers and of the pressures activated on them—is supported by the actual influence which strategic analysis and futures studies did have on public policymaking, both in the United States and in other countries. This influence took place not only on the level of policies, but also on the level of metapolicies, as illustrated by the establishment of special organizations within the central policymaking institutions which engage in strategic studies and futures studies, respectively. Here, the interdependencies between professional and organizational nova-design, on one hand, and influence on actual policymaking, on the other hand, are clearly visible.

6. It is necessary to embed the components within the overall policy sciences framework. Both futures studies and strategic analysis share basic methodological weaknesses. The details of those weaknesses differ, because of the quite different roles in them of imagination versus rational analysis. But both lack an explicated methodology, clarified assumptions, and carefully tried-out methods. It is interesting to observe that, of the two, some parts of futures studies are distinguished by a better worked-out set of methods and even a somewhat more elaborated methodology than strategic analysis is.[3] This may be due in part to the more innovative nature of futures studies which can rely less on established disciplines such as economics than can strategic analysis, and which, therefore, seem to have felt more strongly the need for methodological explication. Whatever the reasons may be, it is the absence of explicated methodologies and methods which must be blamed for many of the weaknesses of both strategic analysis and futures studies, such as narrowness of explored alternatives, neglect of politics, hidden value assumptions, naive tacit theories on various human and social phenomena, and more.[4] In other words, while futures studies and strategic analysis illus-

---

[3]E.g., see Erich Jantsch, *Technological Forecasting in Perspective* (Paris: OECD, 1967); James R. Bright, ed., *Technological Forecasting for Industry and Government: Methods and Applications* (Englewood Cliffs, N.J.: Prentice-Hall, 1968); and Robert U. Ayres, *Technological Forecasting and Long-Range Planning* (New York: McGraw-Hill, 1969). No similar treatments of the methodology, methods, and tools of strategic analysis are available, other than on the more technical level of systems analysis or on specific tools, such as gaming.

trate possibilities to build up components of policy sciences, they also demonstrate the necessity to embed such components within an overall policy sciences framework which provides necessary scientific underpinning. Thus, exploration of the experiences and learning opportunities provided by futures studies and strategic analysis viewed as emerging components of policy sciences seems to support the necessity for new scientific paradigms as a foundation for policy sciences as a whole and for its various subcomponents in particular.

Now that the case has been made, I hope, that policy sciences is needed and possible, we can proceed to the main proposed dimensions of policy sciences.

[4]For some illustrations of fallacies in United States' strategic studies caused largely by the absence of a suitable methodology embedded in a broader framework of policy sciences, see Yehezkel Dror, *Crazy States: A Counterconventional Strategic Issue* (Boston: Lexington Heath, 1971), Chap. 1.

Dimensions
of Policy Sciences

As noted in Part II, some beginnings of policy sciences can be discerned. But we are still far away from a design for policy sciences, which is both compresensive and concrete enough to serve as a taking-off basis for building up policy sciences as an integrated area of knowledge, research, application, teaching, and professionalization.

Part III is devoted to providing the main skeleton of such a design. The fundamental innovations of policy sciences lie in its paradigms, which are presented in chapter 8. Chapter 9 to 12 elaborate the more important new dimensions of policy sciences, by discussing policy analysis, megapolicies, metapolicies, and realization strategies.

Paradigms for Policy Sciences

Policy sciences hardly exists. Therefore, any proposed set of paradigms reflects more the opinions of one author than an established consensus of scholars. Furthermore, when policy sciences develops and reaches an advanced state, it surely will take forms and shapes which are unpredictable. Recognizing the tentative nature and inadequate subjective justification of any set of policy sciences paradigms, I feel, nevertheless, that explicit exploration of the unique paradigms of policy sciences is essential for presenting the basic ideas of policy sciences and for providing the core around which a more detailed design can be constructed.

Explicit consideration of paradigms for policy sciences is all the more necessary because of the revolutionary character of policy sciences in respect to contemporary normal sciences. If the development of policy sciences were to involve only incremental changes within the basic paradigms of contemporary normal sciences, the usual processes of advances in knowledge through slow trial and error and dispersed search within existing disciplines and research structures would suffice. In this case, it might be adequate to use *policy sciences* as a superimposed term covering a broad set of studies, disciplines, and professionals, which cluster around the application of knowledge and rationality to perceived social problems. Indeed, if we were to accept the assumption that all that is needed is advancement of normal sciences, we might broaden the scope of the term *policy sciences* to include all applications of intelligence, the scientific method, and perhaps even common sense[1] to

[1] It is surprising and disturbing how popular the term *common sense* is among scientists, when taking up policy issues. Reasons for this reliance on a meaningless term by scientists probably include (*a*) some feeling that appeal to common sense is democratic; (*b*) the hope that reliance on common sense increases support for a proposal; and (*c*) the absence of a scientific basis for proposals, and therefore a retreat to senseless slogans instead. The fact that much advanced science is counter-common sense makes the reference to common sense in policy proposals by scientists all the more suspicious.

The fuzzy meanings of common sense add to the confusion surrounding the use of this term in policy-oriented pronouncements and even studies. These meanings include (1) what is obvious to the ordinary senses; (2) what is accepted by widespread opinion; and (3) whatever one happens to believe in. In none of these meanings is common sense an acceptable source of knowledge and a basis for recommendation. My suggestion for policy sciences is to avoid this term and to use instead the concepts *tacit knowledge, judgment, widely accepted opinions, subjective view,* etc., whenever appropriate.

human affairs, and thus make the concept of policy sciences quite harmless and completely useless. But I think that something fundamentally new is needed, and that careful and explicit examination of the main paradigms for policy sciences is essential.

Clarification of the basic paradigms of policy sciences is all the more urgent because of the dangers of misuse of the term *policy sciences* as a convenient symbol for whatever activity may seem most important or interesting to the growing number of individuals and institutions who want to devote their efforts to human problems and social issues. There are few ways better designed to ruin the idea of policy sciences before it really gets started than overselling policy sciences by ignoring the limits of science—both inherent and social—and overusing the concept of policy sciences by trying to put into it whatever one regards as needed or useful for human progress.

On the basis of our examination so far, it seems that what needs to be done and can be done is something quite different. In order to make science really relevant for human issues we need a new type of science based on a new set of paradigms. As already noted, this new "policy sciences" is no substitute for contemporary sciences, and especially behavioral sciences and management sciences, which provide essential inputs into policy sciences and the accelerated advancement of which is, therefore, necessary, among other reasons, for the progress of policy sciences. But policy sciences should constitute a new and additional approach to the uses of systematic knowledge, structured rationality, and organized creativity for the conscious direction and transformation of society.

All analogies are misleading when pushed beyond the limits of isomorphism with the investigated phenomenon. Keeping this caution in mind, I shall start the paradigms by first mentioning medicine as a helpful analogue for policy sciences. The differences are great, for instance, in respect to the existence of some clear criteria of "sickness" in the more traditional parts of medicine, while evaluation of societies is largely (with our present state of knowledge) a matter of values and ideologies. But the analogue between policy sciences and medicine is nevertheless a very suggestive one, because of strong similarities in some of the main paradigms and secondary characteristics.[2]

Subject to the above qualifications and hedgings, we will now move on to the paradigms of policy sciences. It does not matter if one specification or another is off its mark. It is the overall *Gestalt* of policy sciences in which we are interested.

It seems to me that the main paradigmatic innovations to be required of

[2]This analogue may provide some justification for the statement by Dubois that "medicine seems best suited to preside in an architectonic way over the development of a new science of human life." Rene Dubois, *Man, Medicine, and Environment* (New York: Praeger, 1968), p. 118.

and expected from policy sciences can be summed up as follows:

1. The main concern of policy sciences is the understanding and improvement of societal direction. Therefore, its main concern is with societal direction systems and, in particular, the public policymaking system. The main test of policy sciences is better policymaking, which produces better policies; these, in turn, are defined as policies which provide increased achievement of goals that are preferred after careful consideration. Policy sciences as such is not directly concerned with the substantive contents of discrete policy problems (which should be dealt with by the relevant normal sciences), but rather with improved methods, knowledge, and systems for better policymaking.

2. Policy sciences focuses on the macro-level, namely, public policymaking systems—subnational, national, and transnational. Subcomponents of the public policymaking system constitute subject matters for policy sciences, because of their roles within the public policymaking system. Therefore, policy sciences deals with individual, group, and organizational decision processes, looking at them from the perspectives of public policymaking. Specific findings of policy sciences are also significant for the improvement of decisionmaking in various units (such as private corporations) independent from their roles, if any, in the public policymaking system. But the perspective of policy sciences is tied in to public policymaking, in the broad sense of that term (which is much more inclusive than, for instance, the term *government*).

3. Policy sciences involves breakdown of traditional boundaries between disciplines, and especially between the behavioral sciences and management sciences. Policy sciences must integrate knowledge from a variety of branches of knowledge and build it up into a supradiscipline focusing on policymaking. In particular, policy sciences is based upon a fusion between behavioral sciences and management sciences. But it also absorbs elements from physical and life sciences, engineering, and other disciplines insofar as they are relevant. To emphasize its multiple components on one hand and its basic unity on the other hand, I propose to use the plural form "policy sciences," but to regard it grammatically as singular.

4. Policy sciences involves bridging the usual dichotomy between pure and applied research. In policy sciences, integration between pure and applied research is achieved by acceptance of the improvement of policymaking as its ultimate goal. As a result, the real world constitutes a main laboratory for policy sciences, and the ultimate test of the most abstract policy sciences theory is in its contribution to the improvement of policymaking. (This contribution can be an indirect and long-range one.) The orientation toward ultimate usefulness for the improvement of policymaking is not to be mixed

up with a pragmatic approach. Thus, policy sciences depends for its development, *inter alia,* on the construction of very abstract theories which have no direct applications to policymaking reality.

5. Policy sciences accepts tacit knowledge and personal experience as important sources of knowledge, in addition to more conventional methods of research and study. Efforts to distill the tacit knowledge of policy practitioners and to involve high-quality policymakers as partners in the upbuilding of policy sciences are among the important characteristics distinguishing policy sciences from contemporary normal sciences, including behavioral sciences and management sciences.

6. Policy sciences shares contemporary sciences' main involvement with instrumental-normative (i.e., prescriptive) knowledge, in the sense of being directed at means and intermediate goals rather than absolute values. But policy sciences is sensitive to the difficulties of achieving "value-free sciences" and tries to contribute to value choice by exploring value implications, value consistencies, value costs, and the behavioral foundations of value commitments. Also, parts of policy sciences are involved in the invention of different alternative futures, including their value contents. As a result, policy sciences constitutes a breach in the solid wall separating contemporary sciences from ethics and philosophy of values, and should build up an operational theory of values (including value morphology, taxonomy, measurement, etc., but not the substantive absolute norms themselves) as a part of policy sciences.

7. Organized creativity, including value invention, constitutes an important component of parts of policy sciences (such as policymaking-system novadesign and redesign, and policy alternative innovation). The encouragement and stimulation of organized creativity are, therefore, a subject for policy sciences and one of its important methods.

8. Policy sciences is very time sensitive, regarding the present as a bridge between the past and the future. Consequently, it rejects the ahistoric approach of contemporary sciences, including most behavioral sciences and management sciences. Instead, it emphasizes historic developments, on one hand, and future dimensions, on the other hand, as central contexts for improved policymaking.

9. Policy sciences is highly sensitive to change processes and dynamic situations. Intense concern with conditions of social transformation and with policymaking on directed change, conditions the basic models, concepts, and methodologies of policy sciences.

10. Policy sciences deals with the contribution of systematic knowledge and structured rationality to the improvement of public policymaking. But policy sciences clearly recognizes the important roles both of extrarational processes (such as creativity, intuition, charisma, and value judgment) and of

irrational processes (such as depth motivation). The search for ways to improve these processes for better policymaking is an integral part of policy sciences, including, for instance, the possible policymaking implications of altered states of consciousness. In other words, policy sciences faces the paradoxical problem of how to improve extrarational and even irrational processes through rational means.

11. Policy sciences both revises accepted scientific principles and basic methodologies and extends them beyond the accepted confines of scientific investigation. Doubts about Occam's razor, the encouragement of apperception, the search for serendipity, social experimentation, much concern with so-called random phenomena and untypical situations, and efforts to invent new social institutions and new laws for social and political behavior—these illustrate the innovative directions of policy sciences' assumptions and methodologies.

12. Policy sciences tries to be self-conscious and to consider its own paradigms, assumptions, tacit theories, infrastructures, and applications as subjects for explicit study and conscious shaping. The constant study, monitoring, and redesign of policy sciences itself are main subject matters of policy sciences. Futhermore, policy sciences should recognize its limitations and explicate the boundaries of its domain of usefulness. The irrelevance of policy sciences for extreme revolutionary endeavors which inherently are hardly feasible and beyond rationality; the inability of policy sciences to deal with deep social transformations which are beyond understanding and direction (e.g., new religions); the inappropriateness of policy sciences for a new *homo superior,* created through genetic engineering, mind-developing drugs, direct man-computer symbiosis, and more; and the dependence of policy sciences on some acceptance of a positive philosophy and belief in rationality —these are some of the boundaries of policy sciences' usefulness. These and other boundaries should be constantly contemplated, studied, and researched, as a main element of policy sciences' self-sophistication.

13. With all its self-sophistication, policy sciences does not accept the take-it-or-leave-it attitude of much of contemporary behavioral sciences, neither does it regard petition signing and similar "direct action" involvements as a policy sciences contribution (in distinction from scientists acting as citizens) to better policymaking. Instead, it is committed to striving for its increased utilization in actual policymaking and to preparing professionals to serve in policy sciences positions throughout the public policymaking system, without letting this sense of mission interfere with a clinical and rational-analytical orientation to policy issues.

14. Despite all innovativeness, policy sciences belongs to the scientific endeavor and must meet the basic tests of science in respect to verification

and validation. Extreme care must be taken not to regard the novelty of
policy sciences paradigms as a license for relaxation of basic scientific standards. Policy sciences should not be judged by the paradigms of contemporary
sciences, but it must meet the basic criteria of all scientific efforts, and, in
addition, the not less demanding tests of saliency to the improvement of
policymaking.

These paradigms constitute the foundation on which the concepts, methodologies, and methods of policy sciences are based. Some of these concepts,
methodologies, and methods are taken over from contemporary sciences;
others are new to policy sciences. But all these concepts, methodologies, and
methods operate in a cluster which is distinctive of policy sciences. Some
dimensions of this cluster are discussed in the following chapters. That discussion will provide many opportunities to concretize diverse implications
of policy sciences paradigms.

CHAPTER 9

Policy Analysis

One of the main dimensions of policy sciences is policy analysis. Policy analysis is based in part on management sciences and, especially, broader versions of systems analysis. Its aim is to provide a heuristic method for identification of preferable policy alternatives.[1]

Identification of preferable policy alternatives involves two distinct but interrelated elements—innovation of new alternatives and selection of the best alternatives from those available. Because of possible conflicts between the more rational components of the selection element and the more extra-rational components of the innovation element, the critical importance of the innovation of new policy alternatives must be emphasized. Especially under conditions of rapid social transformation—which characterize the world today—innovation of new policy alternatives is significantly more important than selection of the relatively best (or least bad) from a series of easily available alternatives, all of which may be inappropriate. The distinction between policy alternative innovation and policy alternative selection has important applied implications—for instance, in respect to building up separate organizations for fulfilling these different functions. Therefore, it is important to bear in mind that I am using the term *policy analysis* to cover both policy alternative innovation and preferable policy alternative selection.

To the basic framework of management sciences (as discussed in chapter 3), policy analysis adds the following components:

a. Penetration into underlying values, assumptions, and tacit theories. These include, in particular, (1) exploration of the values at which policies are directed, (2) long-range goal research, and (3) explicit examination of alternative tacit theories.

b. Consideration of political variables, including (1) political feasibility analysis, (2) examination of social power implications of alternative policies, and (3) analysis of coalition needs and political consensus implications.

[1]My use of the term *policy analysis* as a prescriptive and heuristic aid for identification of preferable policy alternatives must be kept strictly apart from the use of the same term in the behavioral study of policymaking. There, the term refers to analysis of the contents and genesis of actual policies. See, for instance, Lewis A. Froman, Jr., "Public Policy," *International Encyclopedia in Social Sciences,* vol. 13, pp. 204–8; and Ira Sharkansky, ed., *Policy Analysis in Political Science* (Chicago: Markham, 1970).

c. Treatment of broader and more complex issues, involving (1) lower and new scales of quantification (e.g., nominal and non-metric); (2) the necessity to satisfy multidimensional and diverse goals; (3) much primary uncertainty; (4) institutional change as a main mode of policy change; and (5) acceptance of the education of policymakers, sensitization, and long-range impacts as important goals of policy analysis.

d. Main emphasis on policy alternative innovation, involving (1) intense attention to creativity encouragement and input of novel policy designs into the analysis; (2) much reliance on sequential decisionmaking, learning feedback, and social experimentation; and (3) much attention to alternative invention, in addition to alternative synthesis.

e. Much sophistication in respect to social phenomena, for instance, recognition of irrationality, ideologies, mass phenomena, depth variables, and similar nonrational elements as main variables, both of social behavior and of legitimate goal formation; and acceptance of apperception, intuition, serendipity, and experience as valuable sources of knowledge and insight.

f. Institutional self-awareness, for instance, in respect to (1) the necessity for multiplicity and redundancy of analysis and analysis units; (2) the early involvement of politicians, community leaders, etc., in the analytical activities; and (3) the limits of analysis as a perceptive set for cognizing human reality and aspirations.

g. Acceptance of policy "preferization" as the direct goal of policy analysis (in addition to those goals mentioned in paragraph c above, items 4 and 5) instead of "optimization." To "preferize" means to identify a policy alternative which is better than all other known alternatives, but which usually does not satisfy the requirements of "optimality." Often, a preferable alternative is one which achieves min-avoidance—that is, avoidance of the worst of all bad alternatives. Moving from worst to worst plus one can sometimes be a main achievement of policy analysis and a main goal for it.

Building up policy analysis, on the lines indicated above, requires construction of a concept formulation package—through borrowing from other disciplines, through adjusting from available knowledge, and by invention. The concept package should be much more than a useful taxonomy; it must express the main dimensions of policy analysis, its methodology for dealing with policy problems, and its main modes for developing preferable policy alternatives. The concepts serve also as the main anchor points for tools and methods, which serve to make the concepts operational.

Any set of policy analysis concepts is of provisional utility and sure to need early revision. This is particularly true at present with policy analysis being in its first phases of emergence. Any effort to provide a complete and elaborate set of policy analysis concepts is therefore misplaced. But, in order to advance, some starting points must be put forth. These starting point concepts—while provisional and tentative—are, in my opinion, sufficiently operative to concretize the implications of the policy sciences paradigms, to demonstrate the feasibility of developing high-capacity policy analysis knowledge, and to illustrate the required step-level changes in contemporary sciences. They also indicate the present availability of sufficient policy analysis knowledge to make a difference in the quality of policy-making—if that knowledge is put carefully, but with determination, to work.

For these limited purposes, I have selected four policy analysis concepts for a closer look: value sensitivity, operational code assumptions, political feasibility, and policy analysis network. Other interesting concepts include, for instance, value explorations, alternative futures and goals, policy alternative search patterns, leverage envelopes (not points!), unexpected occurrence considerations, sign monitoring and recognition (including "social indicators"), systems delimitation, and many more. But the four selected policy analysis concepts should be sufficient to concretize the idea of policy analysis.

Value Exploration

A main problem cluster of policy analysis involves value questions. This includes the quite well recognized (though unsolved) problem of individual multidimensional utility functions which can neither be aggregated nor compared. But also included are a number of other fundamental issues, which are ignored by large parts of contemporary sciences and policy practices. Among them are the following:

a. Compact ideologies. Much contemporary United States economic and management science value theory assumes trade-offs between different goals, permitting side payments and enabling some uses of Pareto Optimum as a choice criterion. But when compact ideologies exist, values assume more of an "either all-or-nothing" form, trade-offs within dogma-structured goals are difficult, and Pareto Optimum may become logically irrelevant. This is the case, for instance, when an ideology requires someone else to be worse off.

b. Latent values, motives, and needs, which often serve as the main reason for some activities and policies, but which cannot—and sometimes should not—be explicated. Catharsis of emotions, coalition maintenance, ritualistic reinforcement of solidarity, and various symbolic functions—these are some illustrations of important goals for policies that might sometimes be impaired by explication.

c. Irreducible absolute values, which cannot be related to some basic common denominators and which therefore cannot be treated through tradeoff approaches. Especially important are contradictions between absolute values, which pose dilemmas that are universal in real-life policymaking.

  d. The meanings and dimensions of basic social values, such as freedom, democracy, equality, participation, human rights, and the like. It is impossible to take up any complex policy issue without handling these values.

To try and handle these issues, policy analysis must include both substantive material from applied ethics and political philosophy, and advanced methodologies for handling value issues. Fargoing value sensitivity testing, early involvement of legitimate value judges (including participating citizens, in addition to politicians), and bias-reducing redundancy in the analysis process itself—these are some illustrations of possible approaches to the value issues.

Operational Code Assumptions

The concept of "operational code assumptions" belongs to the policy analysis of issues involving interactor relations, in which understanding and predicting the behavior of various multiactors (individuals, groups, organizations, nations, etc.) is of high importance. Especially significant classes of such policy issues are foreign relations and military strategies; but a majority of main social policy issues, if not all, involve many multiactors and therefore require—for better policymaking—prediction of behavior under various assumptions. Hence, operational code assumptions are a very important policy analysis concept.

The concept of operational code is already somewhat developed, though insufficiently used.[2] But its utilization in policy analysis requires further sophistication of the concept, especially in respect to the underlying tacit theories on which efforts to formulate operational codes are based. Much more apperception is needed to bring out the possibilities of explaining given behavior patterns in terms of quite different models or operational codes, and thus avoid the tendency of analysis to view all operational codes as slight variations of those known to the involved analyst from personal experience and those accepted in his culture. This danger is especially acute the more analysts are immersed in rationality approaches, as inability to realize that behavior can follow quite different underlying rules is a highly dangerous trained incapacity, widespread, for instance, in management sciences.

[2]See Alexander George, "The Operational Code; A Neglected Approach to the Study of Political Leaders and Decisionmaking," *International Studies Quarterly* **13**, no. 2 (June 1969): 190–222.

This problem has significant implications for the training and development of analysts, including the need to expose them to direct experiences with different life styles and ideologies. Limiting the discussion to the concepts of policy analysis, I shall emphasize at least the following points:

   a. Operational code assumptions must be multiple, including alternative codes explaining actual behavior. As already noted, care must be taken not to follow Occam's razor and not to accept a priori simpler explanations, such as "economic man models."
   b. Operational code assumptions provide one of the important ports of entry for behavioral sciences knowledge, namely, different models for describing and sometimes explaining and predicting behavior. For instance, organization theory is essential for dealing with the behavior of bureaucratized multiactors, such as governments.
   c. As behavioral sciences knowledge does not provide highly reliable explanations and predictions of behavior, additional sources of understanding must be utilized in policy analysis. These include, for instance, depth psychology and, on a different level, insightful literature and personal experience.
   d. Special care must be taken to overcome cultural bias in dealing with the behavior of actors who do not share the same culture. Thus, in the United States, policy analysis must be on guard against tendencies to regard all behavior as low-risk-taking, without ideological commitments, based on benefit-cost, quasi-economic frames of appreciation and lacking aggressive values.

Political Feasibility

Political feasibility—in relations to policy analysis—can be defined in three closely interdependent ways, as (a) relating to an actor, (b) relating to a policy alternative, and (c) relating to a policy area.

   a. From the point of view of any actor (individual, groups, organization, nation, etc.), political feasibility refers to the space of effective political action within which the actor is able, with a certain probability, to affect reality—including, among other activities, to influence policies and their implementation. In this sense, political feasibility is closely affiliated with the concepts of influence and power. The term *political leverage* can be used to refer to this ability of an actor to influence (among other phenomena) policies and their implementation (including, sometimes, to make and implement policies on his own). A derived term is *political leverage domain,* which refers to the action space within which an actor has political leverage.

 b. Political feasibility as regards a defined policy alternative deals with the probability (or range of probabilities) that within a given time-defined policy alternatives will receive sufficient political push and support to be approved and implemented.

 c. In relation to a policy issue or a policy area, political feasibility refers to the range within which alternatives are politically feasible. The term *political feasibility domain* can be used to refer to this range of alternatives.

Policy analysis is particularly concerned with the prediction of political feasibility in respect to defined policy alternatives and with the identification of political feasibility domains to help guide search for alternatives. The Delphi method can be utilized here as a main technique,[3] as can various other structured consultation forms with politicians and politics-related persons.

Having proposed political feasibility as a policy analysis concept, I would like to add a word of warning, which applies in some degree to all policy analysis and also to policy sciences as a whole. This warning does not relate to the obvious unreliabilities of one proposed method or another. What really worries me is a much more fundamental danger, namely, the danger that every political feasibility prediction—and similar analytical endeavors—tends to ignore the capacities of human devotion and human efforts to overcome apparently insurmountable barriers and to achieve not only the improbable but the apparently impossible. A good policy way may be worth fighting for, even if its political feasibility seems to be nil, as devotion and skillful efforts may well overcome political barriers and snatch victory out of the mouth of political infeasibility. Any political feasibility estimate, however carefully derived and however correct at its time, must therefore be regarded as provisional, sometimes to be taken up as a challenge, rather than accepted as an absolute constraint. In this respect, political feasibility well illustrates the basic orientation of policy analysis—to serve as an aid in high-level heuristic policymaking, but not as a decision-determining algorithm or a set of self-fulfilling predictions.

Policy Analysis Network

A main problem of policy analysis is how to put together its manifold concepts and dimensions and present a coherent and meaningful analytical study of a discrete policy issue. Especially, the absence of commensurate quantitative expressions that can be aggregated into a limited number of easily comprehensible findings poses a major difficulty. One of the integrating concepts

---

[3]See Yehezkel Dror, *Ventures in Policy Sciences* (New York: American Elsevier, 1971) chap. 8.

that permits systematic presentation of a policy analysis study in a form that is meaningful for policymaking is *policy analysis network*. A policy analysis network constitutes a morphological breakdown of a policy issue into a set of interrelated subissues in a form conducive to a decisionmaking program. Such a network presents the logical sequences of the analysis, clearly explicates the various alternative assumptions, and exposes the full complexities of the issue. The main events in the network consist of the subdecisions involved in the policy, the interdependencies between the various subdecisions being represented by the structure of the network. The main features of a policy analysis network should include the following:

a. A full explication of assumptions, value and goal elements, and uncertainties; and a full explication of the utilized techniques and theories, with clear identification of their reliability and validity.

b. The presentation of a range of assumptions, value and goal elements, predictions, techniques, and theories; and an explicit parallel analysis using this range, with clear findings on the sensitivity of conclusions to such differences.

c. A full and explicit development—with alternative assumptions, etc.—of utilized policy analysis concepts, with the help of a multiplicity of techniques. The aggregation of inconsistent findings arrived at by different techniques should be explicated.

d. (Closely related to *b* and *c*): A multiple policy-alternative elaboration, permitting the user of the analytical study, after exposure to the analysis, to select an alternative approximating best his subjective judgment on all elements that are not purely scientific in their nature.

e. The identification of main interconnections with other issues and systems, with some elaboration of possibililities to redefine the problem by changing the delineation of the target system.

f. An open-ended approach, with indication of the main avenues for search for additional alternatives, for changes in underlying megapolicies, and for other approaches to the issue.

g. A provisional and iterative method, with constant movement back and forth between the policy analysis network and relevant reality, so as to continuously revise and advance the policy analysis network.

h. Embedment in the broader perspectives of policymaking, with special attention to improvements in the relevant policymaking system, in evaluation and feedback nets, and in implementation capacities. These improvements should be explored as essential requisites of new policies, as helpful conditions for new policies, and/or as alternatives to immediate changes in policy (as will be discussed soon).

Policy analysis networks can be presented with a variety of visual aids, graphic descriptions, issue mappings, and sometimes computer simulation. The form of a policy analysis network can and should be adjusted to different audiences, ranging from professional analysts to the mass media of communication. Thus, the presentation on television of policy analysis networks of controversial public issues raises fascinating possibilities of significantly improving exposition of problems before the public and trying to advance on the stony road to realizing the requisite of democracy called "enlightened public opinion." Interesting possibilities also exist in respect to utilization of policy analysis networks when teaching citizenship, contemporary problems, and behavioral sciences in schools.

Special attention should be given to develop policy analysis networks directed at politicians and senior executives. In all versions of policy analysis networks, the variance is in degrees of elaboration and details. The basic features, as enumerated above, apply to all form of policy analysis.

In principle, policy analysis provides a heuristic method for identification of preferable alternatives, regardless of the subject matter involved. Policy analysis applies to choice between policy alternatives, between alternative policymaking system designs, between alternative realization strategies, etc. Thus, policy analysis constitutes the main prescriptive method of policy sciences for improving complex decisions.

CHAPTER 10

Megapolicy

Megapolicies involve determination of the postures, assumptions, and main guidelines to be followed by specific policies. They are a kind of *master policy,* clearly distinct from detailed discrete policies, though these two pure types are on a continuum with many in-between cases. Explicit consideration of megapolicies is a major characteristic of policy sciences, differentiating it from contemporary sciences. It is indeed quite amazing to note how neglected megapolicies are, both in behavioral approaches and in prescriptive approaches. The few authors who treat them explicitly do deal only with a narrow range of megapolicy choices and tend to be overinfluenced by one a priori ideology or another, and the socio-economic-political conditions of a particular country and period.

There are a number of megapolicy facets, which form a multidimensional matrix with a large number of cells, presenting the different combinations of various megapolicy facets. If we leave aside the problems of calibration of the different facets—some of which are continuous and some of which have only a few points—there is the possibility of mixed megapolicies, in which, in a given area of policy, different megapolicies can be followed in various policy instances. The choice of whether to follow a pure megapolicy combination (a real cell of the multifacet matrix) or whether to adopt a megapolicy mix (picking different cells according to a predetermined pattern and including as one possibility a random pattern) is itself a main megapolicy decision. There also are empty cells, because of logical contradiction, and nonfeasible cells, because of behavioral conflict. When we consider all this together, the picture becomes very complex but not prohibitively so. It certainly is possible to build up the main outline of a megapolicy matrix, identify essential conditions for each megapolicy, and find out at least some criteria for preference of different megapolicy combinations under various conditions. These are among the important research tasks awaiting policy sciences.

To concretize the concept of megapolicy and to indicate directions for research and possibly for types of contributions to improved policymaking, I will explore twelve main facets of megapolicy:

Overall Goals

The establishment of overall goals to serve as guidelines for large sets of concrete policies is a main requirement of preferable megapolicy.

Before taking up substantive goals for policymaking, a decision must be made on the preferable mix between substantive goals, options, and capacities for the future. This dimension of the overall goals megapolicy facet deals with the choices between definite and concrete goals, a number of defined future choices (e.g., options), and better capacities to achieve as yet undefined goals in the future.

This is an especially important megapolicy choice, because in most more complex policy issues the main results of a policy will occur in the future and sometimes in a quite-distant future. Therefore, such policies should satisfy future values. But future values are very difficult to predict, adding a serious primary uncertainty[1] to the primary and secondary uncertainties of predicting the results of different policy alternatives. In such cases, parts of the overall goals should often be to increase options (that is, leave to the future choice between defined goals) and build up resources for goal setting in the future (that is, prepare resources which permit choice of as yet undefined and unknown goals in the future). The more we expect the future to be different from the present, and the more we would like the future to be different from the present, the more we should be doubtful of present efforts to establish substantive goals for the future. Taking into consideration the rate of social transformation in the contemporary world, the conclusion seems justified that preparation of resources for goal choice in the future should constitute an important component of the overall goals for preferable policymaking.

At the very least, the avoidance of irreversible consequences which may contradict future goals should constitute an important substantive goal for present policymaking. But in considering the irreversibility of consequences, care must be taken not to assume human capacities as fixed. In particular, some of the environmentalists seem to fall into the fallacy of looking on the effects of technology as irreversibly changing the ecology, while ignoring the possibility that new technologies may permit "depollution" of the ecology and construction of an artificial neoecology, which may perhaps be preferred in the future to naturally given environments.

Another main megapolicy choice in respect to overall goals involves the choice between min-avoidance versus achievement of a positively defined state of affairs, as goals for a series of policies. I have already mentioned this point, but because of its applied significance and theoretic significance it bears some repetition.

---

[1]*Primary uncertainty* in my terminology, as already mentioned, is the condition of uncertainty when the dimensions of possible results are unknown. *Secondary uncertainty* is the condition of uncertainty when the dimensions of possible results are known, but their probability distribution is unknown. (The latter is equivalent to the term *uncertainty* in theory of games.)

In some repects, formulation of a goal in the positive or in the negative is a matter of syntax, such as when we talk about "increasing the percentage of employed" or "reducing the percentage of unemployed." But, often, the positive and negative concepts are not located on a single and continuous dimension. For instance, "striving for more health" is only identical in part with "reducing sickness" as public medicine slowly begins to understand. In those many cases in which the positive goals and the negative avoidance goals are not identical, the megapolicy distinction between striving for achievement of more of a positive goal and between striving for reducing the negative as a goal is of much importance. This is especially the case because often it may be easier to achieve agreement on avoidance of a bad situation than on moving toward a good situation. For instance, it is much easier to get agreement and action on avoiding total nuclear war than on realizing a *good* international system (of which nuclear war avoidance is only one characteristic). Therefore, a megapolicy of min-avoidance, in which one tries to move from a worst possible situation to a worst plus one, worst plus two, and so on,[2] is a very important and often optimal possibility, which requires careful consideration.

In regard to the substantive goals component of a preferable overall goals megapolicy, some decision is necessary concerning the relative weight of such basic goals as internal economic development, equality of opportunities, security against attack by other countries, metaphysical values (such as "serving God" or realizing some ideology), and so forth. This requirement is difficult to realize, in part because of the absence of suitable goal taxonomies and value morphologies, and because of the dissonance between political culture and the mechanics of agreement and coalition maintenance, on one hand, and the requirements for goal priority explication, on the other hand. Realizing the necessity to maintain basic consensus and essential social and political coalitions, it seems nevertheless, that some progress on the way to explicit megapolicymaking on overall goals seems essential for improvement of policymaking.

Policy Boundaries

This megapolicy deals with the question, What are the boundaries within which a certain policy is to be confined? In other words, what is the domain of institutions to be considered as appropriate objects for defined policies?

To look at the same megapolicy from a different point of view, the essential issue here is: Which institutions, patterns, arrangements, and so

---

[2]One should note that, because of the stipulated condition that the positive goal is not identical with the avoidance of the negative situation, the set [worst plus *n*] is not identical with the set [best minus *n*], though there may be a shared subset. The idea of min-avoidance constitutes, therefore, a different approach, to be worked out, *inter alia,* in theory of games.

forth should not be impaired or changed through specific policies—either through their utilization as policy instruments or through second-order and third-order consequences of the involved policy? This megapolicy can be formulated as a matter of degrees: some institutions should or may serve as main targets or as main policy instruments within a given policy area; some institutions may be slightly changed to serve as policy instruments or as secondary targets for a policy; while still others must not be touched upon at all.

This megapolicy dimension is closely related, as already indicated, with another one which will be discussed later, namely, the range of policy instruments. Together with overall goals, the boundaries stipulated for a set of policies (or a policy area) do constitute a most basic decision which shapes all features and elements of the relevant policies. Therefore, it is essential not to take any a priori image of policy boundaries for granted, but explicitly to consider and reconsider this megapolicy and decide and redecide it on the basis of careful analysis before and while specific policy issues are taken up.

Preference in Time

The question of the policy target time—When does one wish the main results of policies to be produced?—is another main megapolicy issue. There is a fundamental difference between a policy that wants to achieve certain results *immediately* and a policy that wants to upgrade the capacities of the policy-making system for the next ten to twenty years. This dimension clearly brings out a characteristic shared by all megapolicies, namely, the necessity for iteration and reconsideration of megapolicies in light of detailed policy issues and policy results. Thus, often the politically given desire is for fast results, while a consideration of concrete policy alternatives will make clear that significant results need more time. This conclusion may lead either to reformulation of the time preferences or to "illusionary policy" adoption. The often positive correlation between achievable results and required time, and the sensitivity of this correlation to availability of policy resources and policy instruments are quite clear, and it is very wasteful to relearn through bitter experience what is well known. Nevertheless, exogenous constraints (political feasibility, urgent survival needs, and so on) are often very rigid and impose absolute limits on time availability. Therefore, the early establishment of explicated time preferences in respect to various policies and expected policy outputs is essential as a directive for concrete instances of policymaking. Even more important, the early identification of rigid time constraints is essential for megapolicy consistency, as overall policy goals must often be reformulated because of nonelastic time preferences.

In considering time preferences, it is necessary to get rid of the a priori image of positive, continuous, and linear interest rates. In real-life policy-making, specific results are often required within rather narrow time ranges in the future and are useless if available earlier or later than the designated time range. Therefore, to use for a moment the concept of *interest rates,* despite its frequent inappropriateness for complex policy issues, at least the concept of interest rates must be considered as being sometimes negative, dynamic, and even noncontinuous.

Risk Acceptability

This megapolicy facet involves the degrees of risk to be accepted in respect to given policy issues. Closely related to the next megapolicy dimension, the issue here is mainly whether one is ready to accept the higher risks associated usually with more innovation, or whether one prefers the lower risks often associated with incremental changes. But it is important to bear in mind that the risks of maintaining a contemporary situation or changing it only incrementally may sometimes be higher even than those of fargoing innovation. In theory-of-games terminology, the choices here are between maximax, on one hand, and maximin or minimax, on the other hand. Also involved are preferences between "average expected value," "lottery value," and similar choices between different forms of risk parameters.[3] However abstract, this is a very important choice, especially in view of the tendencies of risk avoidance commonly found in organizations and in many other parts of a policymaking system, on one hand, and the tendencies toward recklessness often found in policy reforms motivated by sweeping social movements and political radical changes, on the other hand. Therefore, explicit judgment on acceptable risks can significantly improve policymaking. Furthermore, the explication of acceptable and preferable risks carries with it important implications for concrete policymaking, by encouraging suitable hedging, contingency planning, and similar risk-absorbing policymaking methodologies.

Incrementalism versus Innovation

This megapolicy facet deals with the choice between various degrees of changes in policies (defined in terms of extent of change, scope of change, and time), ranging from small incremental change of a few policy details over a long period to fargoing, comprehensive, and rapid innovation in policy. One main variable in this choice is risk acceptability: the more innovative a policy is, the higher often are the unpredictable conseqences. What is frequently forgotten is that the higher probability of fargoing improvement in results is also positively correlated with fargoing innovation, the latter offer being an essential (though, by itself, insufficient) condition for the former.

[3]For a stimulating treatment of these and related concepts, see Howard Raiffa, *Decisions Analysis: Introductory Lectures on Choices Under Uncertainty* (Reading, Massachusetts: Addison-Wesley, 1968).

Also, often forgotten is the already-mentioned possibility that the status quo and limited changes in policies may, in some circumstances, be far more risky than even far going policy innovation. Strong organizational tendencies toward incremental change and scarcity of good policy innovations make explicit megapolicymaking on this issue all the more essential for innovative policymaking. Significant and carefully considered innovations (as contrasted with convulsive jumps) are not a natural policymaking phenomenon, and therefore need specific encouragement, which often does not come forth without an explicit megapolicy.

While frequently leading toward more innovation, specific consideration of the pros and cons of innovation in policymaking and of the related risks may also serve to restrain recklessness and encourage a more careful megapolicy. This may involve either a more incremental megapolicy or an effort to combine policy innovations with risk-reducing methodologies, such as pilot experimentation and sequential policymaking (i.e., policymaking by phases, combined with parallel implementation of different alternatives and coupled to constant learning, which permits abandonment of the less promising alternatives after a relatively small investment of resources).

Comprehensiveness versus Narrowness

This megapolicy facet treats the extent to which a policy should deal with a broad range of components or should focus on a few components, or even a single one. Conditioned by the policy boundaries, on one side, and determining the range within which policy instruments may be searched for, on the other side, the degree of comprehensiveness versus narrowness is, nevertheless, a distinct megapolicy facet. Thus, a policy dealing with social welfare will be relatively comprehensive, while a policy dealing only with retraining will be narrower, even if it adopts broader boundaries and includes academic institutions and demand-influencing public images within its scope. It is important to point out that *more comprehensive* does not necessarily mean *more important* or *more significant*. Thus, the narrow policy decision to produce a nuclear bomb was much more significant—in terms of impacts—than very comprehensive policies on foreign relations.

This facet is conceptually important for the additional reason that it categorizes, at least in part, an instance of decisionmaking as policymaking.[4] While the difference is one of degrees, from a certain point on—the exact

[4]Another criterion distinguishing between *decisions* and *policies* is *significance* (subjective and objective) of issues. The extent to which a decision is regarded as a policy is a matter of degrees. My conclusions are insensitive to different perceptions of the borderlines between *policies* and *less-than-policies* decisions. Therefore, this definitional issue is not important for the purposes of this book. For a more detailed treatment, see Yehezkel Dror, *Public Policymaking Reexamined* (San Francisco: Chandler, 1968), esp. pp. 12 ff.

delimitation of which is not important for my present purposes—an issue on the narrower side of this facet will be a decision issue, while an issue on the more comprehensive side will be a policy issue. This megapolicy facet is also important for an additional conceptual purpose, namely, for definition of *planning* as a mode of policymaking. Usually, planning will refer to a policy issue which is comprehensive and longitudinal, that is, which includes a large number of components, to be handled in a synchronized way.

Balance Oriented versus Shock Oriented

The question faced by this megapolicy facet is, to what extent should a policy be directed at achieving given goals through a shock effect on the involved target system, or to what extent should the goals be achieved through an effort to change a number of components together in a mutually coordinated (balanced) way? When a shock megapolicy is adopted, usually the purpose is to achieve longer-range objectives through shocking the target system into a new state of existence, including, hopefully, increased openness to change and propensity to transformation.

This megapolicy dimension is closely related to the comprehensiveness versus narrowness facet, in the sense that only a comprehensive policy can be balance oriented and only a narrow policy can be shock oriented. But it is a separate facet because not every comprehensive policy is or should be balance oriented, and not every narrow policy is or should be shock oriented. This megapolicy facet is especially important because it raises for explicit examination the widely accepted notion that every *good* policy must be balance oriented in the sense of striving for coordinated change of a multiplicity of components. This assumption is strongly reinforced by much of general systems theory, systems analysis, and planning theory. Especially in planning theory, the favorable regard of comprehensive planning (which means both *comprehensive* and *balanced,* as I am using these terms here) leads to widespread fallacies which should be carefully screened for purposes of improved policymaking and which should not exert undue influence on the concepts and prescriptions of policy sciences.[5]

While the idea of balanced policies appeals to our preferences for harmony and is reinforced by a number of tacit and explicit theories (e.g., equilibrium models in behavioral sciences and biological analogues of society), it suffers from a number of serious fallacies. Often very harmful is the innovation-dampening effect of an effort to achieve balanced policies, because innovative alternatives will often appear to be incompatible with balance.[6] Futhermore,

[5]For a detailed treatment, see Yehezkel Dror, *Ventures in Policy Sciences* (New York: American Elsevier, 1971), chap. 11.

[6]Similarly, "overcoordinated" policies lack the randomness necessary for innovation. This important idea is explored in a forthcoming book by Burton Klein.

to preserve balance, we must be able to predict the consequences of directed change—and this, again, pushes us to limit innovations to incrementalism, which provides alternatives, the consequences of which are easier to predict than those of innovative alternatives. When what is aimed at are more fargoing societal changes, shock effects which first disbalance parts of the social system so as to open it up for redesign and novadesign may often be a preferable megapolicy, though admittedly a risky and expensive one. Again, explicit consideration of this megapolicy facet should be useful in at least two directions: (*a*) in helping to overcome the a priori preference for balanced change in situations where policymaking is approached from a conservative point of view, and (*b*) in explicating the risks of shock policies and bringing out the needs for risk-reducing measures in situations where policymaking is approached from a radical point of view.

Relevant Assumptions on the Future

The dependence of preferable policies on a large number of assumptions on the future makes explication of those assumptions into an important need for preferable megapolicymaking.

This problem is especially important in policies with a longer-range time preference, but is also significant when the main time preference lies in the nearer future. The usual practice is to ignore possible alternatives futures and to avoid engaging in systematic efforts to try to study them in connection with discrete policymaking, but rather to assume that what exists now will continue in the future and to engage in arbitrary guesses on futures based on accidental information and personal bias. This is a result of the absence, in most countries, of any efforts to predict alternative futures, and of. the lack of any interconnection between lookout efforts and current policymaking in the very few countries where some lookout mechanisms (in government or outside it) do exist.

Therefore, the establishment of explicit alternative futures assumptions, to serve as contexts for concrete policymaking, is an important contribution to the improvement of policymaking. At the same time, care must be taken to avoid any set of alternative futures from becoming a Procrustean bed, which limits innovation and which restrains concrete policies by too narrow and conservative an image of probable alternative futures. Subject to constant revision of the alternative futures that serve as contexts to be considered in current policymaking on concrete issues, and subject to leeway for innovation in respect to those alternative futures within the analysis of discrete policies, the establishment of an open-ended and constantly updated set of alternative futures to serve as a guideline and a context for discrete policymaking is an important contribution of this megapolicy facet.

Theoretic Bases

The importance of bringing assumptions which are critical for policymaking out into the open, to subject them to conscious reexamination, and if possible, to improve them with the help of systematic knowledge, structured rationality, and organized creativity—this is one of the main intellectual justifications for proposing this megapolicy facet. Psychology and organizational theory bring out the fact that policies are strongly influenced, among other factors, by the tacit theories held by policymakers. *Tacit theory* here means unexplicated believed-in explanations of behavior and other phenomena, in short, subjective images on "what makes the world tick." What distinguishes all tacit theories is that (*a*) by definition they are not subjected to the tests of explicit consideration; (*b*) many of them are rejected by those who hold them, once they are explicated; and (*c*) they lag behind scientific findings, available knowledge, and conclusions of distilled experience. Therefore, this megapolicy facet serves, first, to bring out into the open at least some of the tacit theories underlying policymaking, and, second, to try to improve the tacit theories through conscious consideration and by trying to relate them to explicated theories, available knowledge, and distilled experience.

While setting down megapolicies on theoretic bases of policymaking, much care must be exercised not to increase the rigidity of policymaking. The main idea behind this megapolicy should not be to reduce the range of tacit theories, but should be rather to increase that range. Because of the multidimensional complex nature of most policy-relevant phenomena and the unreliability of relevant knowledge, fixation on any one explanation of reality is a most dangerous dogmatic constraint on the iterativeness and apperception needed for preferable policymaking. Therefore, this megapolicy facet should operate less in the direction of setting down a few explicit theories to displace many tacit theories, but rather in the direction of increasing the diversity of underlying assumptions by explicating the narrowness of commonly held tacit theories and emphasizing the richness of possible alternative explanations and understandings of reality.

Resources Availability

On a different level is the megapolicy facet of resources availability. Here, too, explication is needed and useful to bring up for consideration the often unrealistic hidden assumptions concerning resources which will be available for certain policies, or, even more important, to expose lack of consideration of many cost elements of a proposed policy alternative. This applies not only to money, but—sometimes even more so—to qualified personnel, information, equipment, and the like.

In respect to this megapolicy facet, some clear decisions are called for concerning the resources to be allocated to given policies. Both direct and

indirect costs must be taken into account and the time distribution of resources availability must be worked out, as important constraints on policies.
While iteration may result in some revisions in available resources, more
often constraints on resources are quite rigid, and clear establishment of
policy budget ceilings will have strong influences on policymaking. In particular, it may avoid sudden ruptures of policy implementation because the
tacitly expected resources do not become available. True, sometimes explicit
resources-availability megapolicies may inhibit a policy which otherwise may
have been implemented through piece-by-piece allocation; but I think that,
all in all, more realistic resources allocation will result in more cases of preferable policymaking. This requirement of preferable megapolicymaking on
resources availability is definitely not met by contemporary budgeting practices. Even under a planning-programing-budgeting system, the absence of
multiple-year budgets undermines the function of budgeting as a process
of megapolicymaking on resources availability. Therefore, novel types of
multiple-year budgeting, which involve fargoing changes in present budgeting
arrangements, are necessary for realization of this megapolicy.

The Range of Policy Instruments

This megapolicy facet sums up, in a sense, all other megapolicies, while adding to them an additional perspective. Preferable policymaking means adoption of a mix of policy instruments, which, within the given constraints, provide the highest probability of better approximating the overall dynamic
policy goals. It is therefore in the selection of policy instruments and in their
setting that the megapolicies are transformed into concrete policies. An
essential requisite for selecting a preferable mix of policy instruments and
for their preferable setting is to work out first a list of available policy instruments, with their main characteristics in terms of benefits-costs-risks.

A distinct effort to develop a taxonomy and characterization of policy
instruments as one of the megapolicies is all the more necessary for three
main reasons: (*a*) the tendency to ignore many available policy instruments,
because of tacit theories, limited information, and inertia; (*b*) the potential
benefits of identification or invention of ignored or unknown policy instruments, some of which may prove to be very effective and efficient; and
(*c*) important feedback from policy-instrument evaluation to other megapolicy facets, for instance, by showing the necessity to broaden policy boundaries so as to include additional sets of instruments within the domain of given
policy areas.

Pure versus Mixed Megapolicy

This megapolicy crosscuts all other megapolicies. As already mentioned, this
megapolicy facet deals with the extent to which concrete policies should be

identical in their megapolicies or should adopt a mix of different megapolicies. Concerning mixed megapolicies, various subdimensions of consistency patterns, redundancy possibilities, pluralistic choice, and random selection provide a rich choice, which can be explicated and analyzed. In particular, the advantages of a mix of megapolicies as hedging through redundancy, versus the advantages of consistent megapolicies as achieving synergetic mutual reinforcement, must be carefully considered and evaluated in respect to various policy areas.

In respect to all megapolicies, their interdependence with policy analysis of concrete policy choices, on one hand, and with metapolicies, on the other hand, must be emphasized. Megapolicies should not be regarded as an independent set of variables which shape policies but are insulated from the latter. The opposite is true: policies and megapolicies must constantly interact, both advancing through iteration to a more preferable state. At the same time, megapolicies are also closely interdependent with metapolicies, because only through suitable metapolicy arrangements can megapolicies be established and implemented, and because preferable metapolicies in turn depend on our megapolicy preferences. Specific consideration of megapolicies is essential both for understanding actual policymaking and for improvement of policymaking; but the close interdependencies between policies, megapolicies, and metapolicies should constantly be remembered.

Bearing this remark in mind, we can now proceed to metapolicies.

CHAPTER 11

Metapolicy

Policy analysis and megapolicy are of limited usefulness unless accompanied by improvement of the policymaking system through better *metapolicy,* that is, policy on how to make policy. Therefore, metapolicy is a critical contribution of policy sciences to better policymaking, in addition to constituting an essential dimension of the study and an understanding of policymaking as a behavioral phenomenon.

There would be less need to elaborate this point, were it not that some criticism of the idea of policy sciences has been directed at the proposal to improve policymaking, rather than to focus main attention on concrete and imminent policy issues. Attachment to concrete policy issues can be explained by strong involvement in one burning issue or another, by preference for types of detailed and quantitative data available only in respect to concrete policy issues, by pragmatic tendencies, and sometimes by inability to handle abstract concepts and the long time perspective necessary for consideration of metapolicy and its improvement. Accepted research methods in the behavioral sciences, on one hand, and tendencies to adopt an advocacy stance and become personally relevant, on the other hand, combine and explain the resistance to the idea of metapolicy, especially by some "concerned" behavioral scientists.

My main response to such doubts about metapolicy is that very little can be done to improve policies by more than incremental bits without reforming the policymaking system, that is, without considering and improving metapolicy. Furthermore, efforts to improve metapolicies are often the best avenue to utilize limited resources so as to achieve significantly better policies.

The reasons for this position can be summed up as follows, going from the particular to the general:

1. Innovative policy recommendations, including those coming from policy analysis and from other policy sciences dimensions such as megapolicy, have little chance of being carefully considered, adopted, implemented and revised unless the policymaking system develops new capacities for creativity, consideration, implementation, and feedback. Also required are significant relaxations of present constraints on policies, including, in particular, political and organizational constraints. New patterns of decisionmaking are needed, which in turn require changes in most of the elements of the policymaking system,

74

including personnel, structure, "rules of the game," equipment, and, perhaps most important of all, "policymaking culture."

2. Because of the interdependencies between different policies, the improvement of individual policies is of limited utility unless synergetically related to suitable adjustments in other policies. This requires improvements in the output of the policymaking system in respect to a large number of policies, which in turn can be achieved only through changes in the performance of the policymaking system as a whole.

3. A single policy decision, even an important one, is after all only a minor event in the ongoing process of issue recognition, policymaking-resources allocation, policy decision, implementation, various forms of feedback, contextual change, issue reformulation, and so on. In other words, policymaking is an ongoing activity. Therefore, improving the overall policymaking capacity of a policymaking system is more important than improving any single policy. In cost-effectiveness terms, investing limited resources into improving the policymaking system rather than into improving a single policy is often much more effective in terms of resulting in better policies.

These three reasons together constitute, I think, an overwhelming case for improving the policymaking system, without neglecting current policy issues, both as a main requisite for getting single policies improved by more than incremental bits, and, more important, for achieving long-range improvements in respect to as yet unforseen, but surely critical, policy issues of the future.

The problems of megapolicy can best be considered within a general systems theory frame of appreciation. Adopting a very simple general systems model, we can regard policymaking as an aggregative process in which a large number of different units interact in a variety of part-stabilized but open-ended modes. In other words, policy is made by a system, the policymaking system.

This system is a dynamic, open, nonsteady state and includes a large variety of different, changing multirole components interconnected in different degrees and through a multiplicity of channels; it is closely interwoven and overlapping with other systems (e.g., the productive system, the demographic-ecological system, the technological and knowledge system, and the cultural system), and it behaves in stochastic ways which defy detailed modeling.

Even such a simple perspective of the public policymaking system leads to three important conclusions in respect to metapolicies:

1. As policy is a product of complex interactions between a large number of various types of components, similar changes in the output (or "equifinal states") can be achieved through many alternative variations in the components. This means, for our purposes, that different combinations of a va-

riety of improvements may be useful in achieving equivalent changes in the quality of policymaking. This is a very helpful conclusion, because it permits us to pick out of a large repertoire of potentially effective improvements those that are more feasible under changing political and social conditions. This view also emphasizes the open-ended (or, to be more exact, "open-sided") nature of any search for improvement suggestions: there is, in principle, unlimited scope for adventurous thinking and invention.

2. A less optimistic implication of a systems view of policymaking is that improvements must reach a critical mass in order to influence the aggregative outputs of the system. Improvements that do not reach the relevant impact thresholds will, at best, be neutralized by countervailing adjustments of other components (e.g., a new planning method may be reacted to in a way that makes it an empty ritual) or, at worst, may in fact reduce the quality of overall policy (e.g., through possible boomerang effect, reducing belief in the capacity of human intelligence—with a possible retreat to some types of mysticism, leader ideology, etc.—or by implementing wrong policies more efficiently, thus reducing an important social protective mechanism—inefficiency as diminishing the dangers of implementation of wrong decisions and as permitting slow and tacit learning).

3. The third, and again optimistic, implication of a systems view of policymaking is that, thanks to the interactions between different system components, it may be possible to achieve the threshold of overall system output effects through a combination of carefully selected changes in controlling subcomponents, each one of which by itself is incremental. In other words, a set of incremental changes in systems components can in the aggregate result in fargoing system output changes. Therefore, because we are speaking about changes in the policymaking system, there may be a good chance that a set of relatively minor and quite incremental changes in the policymaking system will permit—through multiplier effects—far-ranging innovations in the specific policies made by that system. This possibility is of much practical importance, because of the much greater feasibility of incremental change than of radical change in the United States and many other countries (though, I think, the readiness to innovate is increasing, as a result of the shock effects of highly perceived crises symptoms).

Further to illustrate the subject matter of megapolicy, I shall mention, in no particular order, a few tentative subjects for research and improvement:[1]

1. Systematic evaluation of past policies in order to learn from them for

[1]For examination of the policy sciences theoretic bases of some of these recommendations, see Yehezkel Dror, *Public Policymaking Reexamined* (San Francisco: Chandler, 1968), Part V, pp. 217 ff. For operational elaboration of some of these recommendations, see Yehezkel Dror, *Ventures in Policy Sciences* (New York: American Elsevier, 1971).

the future. For instance, methods and institutions to provide an independent audit of the results of legislation every five years are both urgently needed and realizable with presently available knowledge.

2. Better consideration of the future. Special structures and processes to encourage better consideration of the future in contemporary policymaking are needed. These include, for instance, dispersal of various kinds of lookout organizations, units, and staff throughout the societal direction systems, and utilization of alternative images of the future and scenarios in all policy considerations.

3. Methods and means to encourage creativity and invention in respect to policy issues. These include, for instance, no-strings-attached support to individuals and organizations engaging in adventurous thinking and organized dreaming; avoidance of their becoming committed to present policies and establishments; and the opening up of access channels for unconventional ideas to high-level policymakers and to the public at large. Creativity and invention may also be influenced within policymaking organizations by institutionally protecting innovative thinkers from organizational conformity pressures. Also requiring careful study are creativity-amplifying devices and chemicals and arrangements for their possible use in policymaking.

4. Improvement of one-person-centered high-level decisionmaking. Even though of very high and sometimes critical importance, one-person-centered high-level decisionmaking is very neglected by management sciences and behavioral sciences alike. This in part is due to difficulties of access and to dependence of such decisionmaking on the personal characteristics and tastes of the individual occupying the central position, which makes it very difficult to study and improve such situations. Neglect of the study and improvement of one-person-centered high-level decisionmaking is also largely a result of lack of suitable research methods, conceptual frameworks, and prescriptive models in contemporary sciences. With the help of novel policy sciences approaches, one-person-centered high-level decisionmaking can be improved. Thus, many conditions of better decisionmaking can be satisfied by a variety of means, some of which may often fit the desires of any particular decisionmaker; for example, information inputs, access of unconventional opinions, feedback from past decisions, and alternative predictions can be provided by different channels, staff structures, mechanical devices, communication media, and so on. This multiplicity of useful arrangements provides sufficient elasticity to fit the needs, tastes, preferences, and idiosyncrasies of most, if not all, top decisionmakers.

5. Development of politicians. The idea of developing the qualifications of politicians is regarded as quite taboo in Western democratic societies. Certainly it is not faced in management sciences nor in modern political sciences.

But this is not justified. The qualifications of politicians can be improved within the basic democratic tenets of free elections and must be improved so as to increase the probabilities of good policymaking and to build a new symbiosis between power and knowledge. Thus, for instance, politicians need an appreciation of longer-range political, social, and technological trends, need capacities to consider megapolicies, and should be able critically to handle complex policy analysis networks. One possible approach to the problem is to encourage entrance into politics of suitable, qualified persons and to vary the rules of presentation of candidates to permit better judgment by the voter. Other less radical proposals are to establish suitable programs in graduate schools where many future politicians study (such as law schools) and to grant to elected politicians (e.g., members of a state legislature) a sabbatical to be spent in self-developing activities, such as studying and writing. Suitable programs can be established at universities and at special centers for active politicians to spend their sabbaticals in a productive and attractive way. (I will return to this subject in chapter 14).

6. Radical changes in the school teaching of "good citizenship" and current affairs subjects. In the longer run, better preparation of the citizen for his roles in policymaking is of critical importance. A first and relatively easy step to meet urgent needs is far-reaching change in the teaching of all "good citizenship" subjects in the elementary and high schools—in the direction of developing individual judgment capacities, learning information search and evaluation habits, and increasing tolerance for ambiguities, as well as readiness to innovate. Intensive use of new teaching methods, such as gaming and projects, and full exposition to contradicting points of view may be helpful in the desired directions. Also to be studied are possible needs and ways for reform of the teaching of various traditional subjects (and of relevant teacher preparation) so as to introduce pupils early to a policy-oriented view of reality and problems.

7. Establishment of a multiplicity of policy research organizations to work on main policy issues. Some of these policy research organizations should work for the central government, some for the legislature, and some for the public at large, diffusing their findings through the mass media of communication. Some policy research organizations should also operate on the multinational and the international level.

8. Development of extensive social experimentation designs and of institutions able to engage in social experimentation (including reconsideration of involved ethical problems). It seems quite clear that social experimentation is essential for finding solutions to present and emerging social issues. Careful social experimentation requires invention of new research designs and of new legal-political arrangements. Also important and very difficult

is the requirement for a political and social climate in which careful research and experimentation on social institutions is encouraged.

9. Institutional arrangements to encourage "heresy" and the consideration of taboo policy issues, such as the possibilities of long-range advancement of humanity through genetic policies and of changes in basic social institutions, such as the family.

These nine examples are intended to serve only as illustrations. To invent novel megapolicies, to identify alternative, preferable metapolicies, and to help in their realization in concrete policymaking systems—these are among the tasks of policy sciences.

CHAPTER 12

Realization Strategy

One of the unique paradigms of policy sciences is that it has an intense commitment to the improvement of policymaking, that is, to achieving actual impact on reality. Therefore, means and ways actually to improve policymaking through the application of policy sciences and through the realization of policy sciences recommendations are themselves an important dimension of policy sciences. This is the subject matter of realization strategy.

Viewed as a dimension of policy sciences, realization strategies involve three levels of study and action: (1) understanding the dynamics of change in respect to policymaking, (2) identifying change instruments in respect to policymaking, and (3) building up policy sciences so as to operate through these change instruments in the direction of policymaking improvement.

To understand the rules of change of the policymaking system, on both the change level and the ultrachange level (that is, on the level of changes of the rules of change themselves), is a task for behavioral research, augmented by some of the particular tools of policy sciences, such as explication of tacit knowledge and experience of policy practitioners. The identification of change instruments involves a search for variables which influence the policymaking system and which are susceptible to setting and resetting. Building up policy sciences so as to influence the policymaking system to utilize the change instruments involves building up personnel, institutions, communication means, and so forth, through which the ideas and recommendations of policy sciences can be conveyed to the policymaking system, be integrated into it, and serve to change policymaking in preferable directions.

Before I further explore the realization dimension of policy sciences through examination of some issues, some examination of the involved moral assumptions is necessary. I leave for the Epilogue the fundamental moral problem of policy sciences, namely, its possible misuses to advance bad and even catastrophic goals. Here I want to focus on another moral issue of policy sciences, which is aggravated by my concern with realization strategies —that is, with strategies explicitly designed to increase the influence of policy sciences and, therefore, policy scientists—on policymaking. This issue is the old one of "rule by scientists." A superficial view may lead one to conclude that my conception of policy sciences is a step on the way to a total change in government, in which the policy scientists will serve as Plato's guardians, taking over government.

This is a completely mistaken conception. I do think that a need exists for fargoing reform of government, including a new division of functions and power between different groups and professionals, within the basic tenets of democracy. As will be elaborated in chapter 16, policy sciences, when developed, will require and bring about a number of changes in politics—but none of them will impair any basic tenet of democracy and most of them will not even change many of the less basic rules of contemporary politics. The very diversity of policy scientists in personalities, values, and backgrounds and the dispersal of policy scientists throughout the societal direction system (which, as we shall soon see, is one of the basic realization strategies) by themselves are sufficient to lay to rest, as unwarranted, fears of a new type of rule by policy scientists. To this the by now redundant point should be added that, while policy sciences has an important contribution to make to the improvement of policymaking, it deals only with a few aspects of policymaking, excluding many even more important ones. The best analogue, in some respects, is economics: while economic knowledge has significantly influenced economic policymaking and while economists, as individuals, have much influence on concrete policies, nevertheless—thanks to the variety of opinions among economists and their dispersal throughout the societal direction system—their power and influence does not aggregate other than in influencing the quality of economic policymaking in some directions and under some conditions through providing an input of knowledge, concepts, and prescriptive models.

Recognition of the moral issues of policy sciences and confrontation of them are essential for preserving a sharp distinction between realization strategies as a dimension of policy sciences directed at improving policymaking and the danger of the policy scientist becoming a new type of Machiavellian alchemist. Therefore, I wanted to mention these moral issues, before taking up some particular realization strategies, to illustrate the scope of this dimension of policy sciences.

To exemplify the realization strategy dimension of policy sciences, let me concisely mention a few particular realization strategy facets:

Communication

Communication of the findings of policy sciences to policymakers is a critical issue of realization strategy. The absence of books and texts in behavioral sciences and management sciences alike, which are mainly written for public policymakers (as contrasted with texts written for business managers), is striking. It illustrates the neglect of the communication issue between policymakers and contributors of scientific and professional knowledge to policymaking—an issue which has to be handled by policy sciences as a very important aspect of realization strategies.

The communication issue transgresses beyond the preparation of texts, analyses, and recommendations in a written form which is relevant to policymakers, which is comprehensible to them, and which combines complete intellectual honesty with convincing representation of the more reliable findings and analyses. Beyond written communication—which is important and needs significant improvements—other media of communication are highly significant. Thus, both structured and unstructured personal interaction between policy scientists and policymakers is essential for communication of policy sciences to policymakers. Briefings, informal mixing in various social contexts, and perhaps some personnel interchange—these are some illustrations of relevant possibilities.

Education of Policymakers

Communication in the full sense of the term involves more than the transmission of information; it involves the capability of the receiver to absorb the information and act upon it, if he so desires. Therefore, communication and education of the policymakers are closely interdependent and synergetically interrelated. Conveyance of the basic frames of appreciation of policy sciences to policymakers is essential, not only in order to permit policy sciences to influence policymaking, but also in order to limit such influence and inhibit bad policy sciences studies from having undue impact on policymaking. A main purpose of education of policymakers in this context (which is only a subcomponent of education of policymakers for better policymaking, as a metapolicy recommendation) is to enable them critically to consider policy sciences findings, with special sensitization to the pitfalls of policy analysis and megapolicy recommendations. The design of educational programs for policymakers, which can range from one or two study days to a sabbatical year, is therefore an additional important realization strategy for policy sciences.

Indirect Impact on Policymakers

The indirect approach is very important in order to influence policymakers. What I have in mind here is sensitization of various interest groups and opinion shapers to the potentials of policy sciences, so as, in turn, to exert influence on the policymakers to increase their demand for policy sciences inputs. This, as we shall see later on, is also important for strengthening the democracy-augmenting effects of policy sciences, if properly used. As an operational illustration, short courses in policy sciences for newspaper correspondents and presentation of policy analysis networks of acute problems on television—these can serve as important means to sensitize the public to the potentials of policy sciences and indirectly to increase the influence of policy sciences on actual policymaking.

Dispersal of Policy Scientists throughout the Societal Direction System

In order to achieve impact on actual policymaking, policy sciences must be introduced into the innermost decisionmaking and policymaking processes. Policymaking is a diffuse process, in which a large number of units are involved. (Those units constitute the public policymaking system, and—if we want an even larger framework—the societal direction system.) Therefore, it is necessary for policy scientists to be dispensed throughout the various components of the policymaking system. This is necessary not only in order to increase the aggregate impact of policy sciences on policymaking but also to insure the redundancy which is essential to reduce bias, to hedge against possible inbuilt mistakes of policy sciences, and to assure policy sciences contributions to policymaking which are in accord with the precepts of pluralistic democracy.

New Organizations

Dispersal throughout the public policymaking system, as mentioned in the last paragraph, is closely related to the need for new types of organizations, which fit the needs of policy sciences and, especially, the requirement of impact on actual policymaking. Bcause of the heterogeneity of components of the policymaking system, on one hand, and because of the variety of policy sciences contributions to policymaking, on the other hand, a large range of different organizations is required. These range from a new role conception of "policy analyst" within a governmental agency, to independent policy research organizations, which work for the public at large or for different components of the public policymaking system. Whatever the specific features of any such organization may be, they must carefully balance the contradictory requirements of close rapport and contact with policymakers versus sufficient insulation from pressures to preserve the professional independency essential for worthwhile policy sciences work. The preferable balance between these contradicting requirements varies: an individual policy analyst working in close relationship with a senior policymaker will pay more attention to his continuous interface with the policymaker, while an independent policy research organization will emphasize more the needs of independent high-quality work. But the individual policy analyst must also preserve a minimum of professional independence; otherwise, he loses his characteristics as a policy scientist and his contribution to policymaking becomes distorted. And the policy research organization must preserve close communication and access to main policymakers; otherwise, too, its contributions to policymaking become distorted, though in a different way, and its chances to influence actual policymaking are much reduced. The establishment of a variety of organizational setups for policy scientists constitutes, in all its forms, a main requisite for actual impact of policy sciences on policymaking.

Timing

The feasibility of realization of policy sciences proposals—especially on the megapolicy and metapolicy level—depends significantly on timing. Feasibility changes with crises and crises perceptions; therefore, having ready a number of improvement proposals, which most of the time are unfeasible but may become feasible as a consequence of crises that result in increased propensity to change, constitutes a main realization strategy for policy sciences thus emphasizing the need for policy sciences to work out a large range of proposals for the improvement of policymaking, even if many of them seem to be nonfeasible. A time perspective, which realizes the changing nature of feasibility constraints and recognizes the long-range educational effects of good proposals—which themselves change feasibility constraints—is essential here.

Institutional Development Studies and Methods

A main need is the design of methods and tools for institutional development, as illustrated by some contemporary organizational development approaches,[1] but on a larger scale and with a larger variety of techniques and methods. How can complex institutions, such as main components of the policymaking system, be developed and improved? is a main issue for research by policy sciences, in order to supply essential realization strategies. What is really needed is an "intervention theory" in respect to the policymaking system.

Stoic Commitment

In order to have any chance whatsoever of useful impacts on policymaking, policy scientists must have an intense moral commitment to try to improve policymaking. At the same time, chances for success are low. At the very best, changes in policymaking will be slow, inconsistent, and sporadic. Even slow and minor changes in the quality of policymaking are a tremendous achievement when compared with the history of human stupidity, but the rate of progress—however significant—will hardly satisfy the hopes and ambitions of policy scientists. Therefore, they are going to be very frustrated persons, with all the accompanying dangers of getting cynical and apathetic, on one hand, or of despairing of their role as contributors of policy sciences to policymaking and jumping to the different role of activists, on the other hand. A stoic view of reality combined with missionary devotion to the

[1]See Chris Argyris, *Intervention Theory and Method: A Behavorial Science View* (Reading, Mass.: Addison-Wesley, 1970).

improvement of policymaking is required from policy scientists, in order to achieve long-range and insistent impact on policymaking.

These are some of the principal realization strategies of policy sciences. All these realization strategies—together with better policy analysis, mega-policies, and metapolicies—depend on research in policy sciences, teaching of policy sciences, and professionalization of policy sciences. To these I now turn.

PART IV

The Advancement
of Policy Sciences

The dimensions of policy sciences provided a general perspective and supplied some main components for the design of policy sciences. But their exploration is only a provisional starting point. To build up policy sciences, the necessary knowledge must be developed, scholars and researchers in policy sciences must be prepared, and policy sciences professionals must be educated. One of the characteristics of policy sciences is the close interdependence between these three directions of activities, namely, research, teaching, and professionalization. In this part, some main issues of policy sciences research, teaching, and professionalization are explored—with special attention to the interdependencies and mutual relationships among them.

CHAPTER 13

Research in Policy Sciences

Policy sciences is, as yet, in an embryonic state. Its successful birth and rapid maturation depend largely on intense and broad research. This research must express and fit the specific paradigms and unique needs of policy sciences while also achieving excellence by the standards of science as a whole. As already indicated—exactly because of the fargoing ambitions of policy sciences and because of the innovative nature of its paradigms, methodologies, and some of its methods—the standards of research in policy sciences must be all the more strict and pedantic, though different from those of normal science.

Research in policy sciences, as in all disciplines, is bifurcated into two main directions: (1) research into the contents of policy sciences, such as policy analysis, megapolicy, metapolicy, and realization strategy; and (2) inner-directed research on policy sciences itself, its methods, methodologies, organization, professional structure, and so on. Much of the content of policy sciences is essentially methodological. Therefore, overlappings and interdependencies between content research and inner-directed research are more pronounced in policy sciences than in other disciplines. To this characteristic of policy sciences research, another one must be added, namely, the importance of research related to concrete policy issues. This third main line of policy sciences research closely conditions the first two and interacts with them intensely.

The main goal of policy sciences, as stated over and over again, is the improvement of policymaking—in the sense of making better policies, that is, policies which achieve more effectively and more efficiently goals and values, after full value consideration. The test of better policymaking being the derivation of better policies, as defined just now, it is inappropriate and impossible to divorce studies on the improvement of policymaking from studies for the improvement of concrete policies. To a large extent, the concept of policy analysis serves to tie in policy sciences as a whole with the improvement of discrete policy decisions. But the close interrelationships between better metapolicies, better megapolicies, better policy analysis, better realization strategies, and better discrete policies must be emphasized. The quality of concrete policies being, both in the short and in the long range, the main target, object, and goal of policy sciences, real-life policymaking serves necessarily as a main laboratory for policy sciences. Involve-

89

ment in the study of real-life policy issues (in partnership with the relevant normal sciences) is, therefore, an essential characteristic of policy though not a main feature of the paradigms of policy sciences as such. (To exercise policy sciences terminology, it is a main megapolicy for policy sciences research.)

Research activities are closely related to research organizations. In respect to policy sciences, the specific features of policy sciences research are highlighted and put into perspective by an examination of the unique organization needed for policy sciences research and its main characteristics.

The requirement to combine study of concrete policy issues with policy sciences research proper—that is, studies which focus on metapolicies, megapolicies, policy analysis, realization strategies, and inner-directed issues of policy sciences—has main implications for the preferable organizational location of policy sciences research. In particular, the need to combine research on concrete policy issues with policy sciences research leads to the conclusion that special policy research organizations serve as a preferable location for research in policy sciences. This does not imply that individual scholars or small groups of scholars cannot engage in highly significant policy sciences research on their own or within traditional academic structures; but a main locale for policy sciences research, and one which is unique to policy sciences research, is special policy sciences research organizations.

The main characteristics of policy research organizations, which make them preferable locations for policy sciences research and therefore illuminate the latter's special characteristics, can be summed up as follows:

Policy-Improvement Oriented

The mission of policy research organizations is to contribute to the improvement of policymaking, by direct contributions to concrete policy problems, by contributions to longer-range policy issues, and by the building up of policy sciences. The time perspective can be a mixed one, with more or less emphasis on shorter-range contributions and longer-range contributions, respectively—the emphasis varying between different policy research organizations and between different subunits and projects within policy research organizations. But the ultimate test of policy research organizations is contribution to the improvement of policymaking. This is their mission and this is their *raison d'être*. Therefore, in policy research organizations, no distinction between pure and applied research exists. Research can be more theoretic or more pragmatic, more imaginative or more analytical, shorter range or longer range, narrower or more comprehensive—but it is always ultimately directed at contributing to the improvement of policymaking.

Interdisciplinary

Because of the multidisciplinary bases of policy sciences—and because of the complex nature of real policy issues, which overlap with the domain of interest of many disciplines—policy research organizations must be interdisciplinary in their composition; that is, the core staff should come from different disciplines of origin. In particular, staff members from the behavioral sciences and from the management sciences are essential. But also required are staff members who come from the physical and life sciences, from history, from law, from philosophy, and more. Furthermore, a number of staff members with significant practical experience in policymaking are essential. At the beginning, such a staff operates as a multidisciplinary one. With time, under the impact of common work which focuses around concrete policy issues and defined policy sciences research subjects—and with suitable intellectual guidance and leadership—this staff becomes interdisciplinary. Given the existence of policy sciences, the staff will continue to develop more and more in the direction of becoming a true supradisciplinary policy sciences staff. Preferably, a staff which is trained in policy sciences (if available) should constitute the core of policy research organizations—but always in some combination with scholars coming from a variety of disciplines, so as to maintain fruitful and stimulating interaction between policy sciences, on one hand, and the various policy-relevant normal disciplines, on the other hand, and so as to supply a variety of knowledge and approaches on a continuous basis.

Critical Size

The professional staff of a policy research organization must be large enough to permit intense depth study of significant problems, application of different disciplines of knowledge, and diversity in approaches. The staff should also be large enough for simultaneous study of a number of problems, to permit efficient study scheduling, provide cross-fertilization between different studies, assure significant contributions to policymaking, and hedge against the unavoidable abortion of some studies. On the basis of relevant experience, it seems that a full-time staff of twenty to twenty-five highly qualified multidisciplinary professionals is the minimum required critical mass. Some of that staff can also engage in limited academic activities, but, in the main, the professional staff should be full time. Consultants, brain trusts, part-time researchers, and so on can be added to the full-time staff.

Staff Characteristics

The core staff must be of the highest academic quality, not less so than the level of senior university professors (senior in the intellectual sense—a chronologically young staff is often preferable for policy research organizations, being more open-minded than persons who are oversocialized in the paradigms and patterns of normal sciences). But it is not sufficient to recruit a high-quality staff; constant steps further to develop that staff are essential.

Minor steps include close involvement of the staff members in various professional activities, opportunities for exposure to different approaches and cultures, movement between different types of issues, constant learning activities, and so forth. More important is the need to prevent getting stale in policy research. This implies, I think, movement between policy research organizations to academic university institutions, on one side, and to other policy sciences roles and even policymaking and policy-implementing line functions, on the other side. Therefore, tenure should be avoided at policy research organizations. The majority of persons give most of what they can provide at a policy research organization during four or five years. Then they should move over to some other function within the domain of policy sciences (and outside it), returning again after a couple of years—if they wish to do so—to a policy research organization.

Administrative Facilities

Too mundane for specific mentioning, were it not for the frequent neglect of this requirement in reality, in particular at universities, is the necessity for excellent administrative facilities. The time of high-quality staff is the scarcest of all resources for policy research. Therefore, administrative facilities and services should be made essentially a "free good" so as to permit maximum utilization of that scarcest resource of all—the time of the professional staff—for its main mission of policy research. Computer time, secretarial facilities, research assistants, communication and travel facilities, libraries and collection of working papers—all these should be available up to a saturation point, to permit exclusive attention by the professional staff to policy research under conditions of maximum convenience.

Confidential Relations with Policymakers

An essential requisite for useful policy research is confidential relations with relevant policymakers. This is necessary, (a) to permit access to necessary data; (b) to permit constant interface during ongoing research—to improve the research, to educate the policy scientists, and to educate the policymakers; and (c) to permit communication of research findings, with some probability of impact on real policymaking. The closeness of contacts with policymakers and the freedom of access depend on the location of a particular policy research organization within the societal direction system and on the constitution of its main clientele—ranging from a specific top-level group of policymakers to the public at large. But significant access to some policymakers is usually essential for useful policy research. Some problems can be handled with less data or with publicly available data; but, for real impact on policymaking, a great deal of access to policymakers is usually (though not always) necessary.

This access involves more than the ability to get information. To achieve impact, to maintain morale in the policy research organization (and in many other forms of policy sciences research), and to permit learning through feedback, more is needed: the relations between policy research organizations (and some other forms of policy sciences research) and policymaking should motivate the latter to listen, consider, and respond to the main studies produced by the policy research organization. (These four requirements from policymaking for good policy sciences research—to inform, to listen, to consider, and to respond—also constitute important implications of policy sciences for politics. I will return to them in chapter 16.)

Freedom of Research

An even more important requirement than the last one, and one which is in strong contradiction with it, is the requisite of research freedom. Not only must a policy research organization be free to study problems in the way it considers best, but it must also be free to reformulate problems and even to pick those problems from a broad policy area which it regards as most significant and which also interest its research staff. Trying to satisfy both requirements involves necessarilly hard compromises. Some policy research organizations will satisfy more the requirement of access to policymakers with some restraints in its freedom of research; other policy research organizations will enjoy less access to policymakers, but nearly complete freedom of research. Redundancy being necessary, it is useful for different policy research organizations to occupy different positions on the continuum between the two extremes. But every policy research organization must preserve at least a minimum of access to data and policymakers and a minimum of research freedom—the latter "minimum" being quite a great deal—so as to preserve the professional standards of policy sciences and to protect the quality of policy sciences contributions to better policymaking.

Time Availability

To permit penetration into complex issues (and the accumulative building up of policy sciences), policy research organizations require time. Furthermore, in order not only to have the time but to feel secure in developing longer-range studies, multiple-year assurance of resources is necessary. Therefore, policy research organizations should preferably enjoy budgetary security for three to five years at a stretch. Here, again, a variety of arrangements is desirable and possible, with some policy research organizations focusing more on short-range issues, while most of them should engage in longer-range studies. Some dependence on resource allocations by the policymakers as clients may be useful, in order to assure sufficient efforts in policy research organizations to keep in contact with policymaking reality and to try to make their studies salient to the needs of policymaking. At the same time, protection from short-range financial pressures is essential to achieve the necessary freedom of research, the required time perspective, and a suitable research climate.

Organizational Climate

More difficult to specify, but, nevertheless, very important, is the requirement for a suitable organizational climate. The organizational climate and work patterns of policy research organizations must encourage frank mutual criticism, uninhibited creativity, breakdown of disciplinary boundaries, continuous learning by staff, and constant freshness of approach. Distinctions must be made between policy research organizations which focus more on the creation and invention of new policy alternatives and policy research organizations which focus more on the screening of alternatives and selection of preferable ones. But the basic requirement for suitable organizational climate is shared by all policy research organizations, as an essential requisite of policy sciences research.

Science Based

Policy research organizations are different from advocacy groups, social prophets, and utopia writers. The specific role of policy research organizations —which in some opinions may be less important than that of the other just-now mentioned functions, but is the one with which policy sciences and policy sciences research are concerned—is to improve policymaking through contributing systematic knowledge, structured rationality, and organized creativity. It is this policy sciences foundation which characterizes policy research organizations and their contributions to policymaking.

Policy research organizations are a fascinating subject, much neglected in organization theory, political sciences, and democratic theory alike. Among the subjects which should be included in a fuller discourse on policy research organizations are problem search patterns, work methods, forms of output, quality controls, staff recruitment and development, formal relations with clients, and many more. But the above-mentioned ten characteristics are sufficient for my present purpose, namely, to provide some "feeling" for the preferable features of policy research organizations as an indication of the flavor of policy sciences research. The one additional issue which I want to mention briefly concerns the formal location of policy research organizations in relation to policymaking organizations, on one hand, and universities, on the other hand.

As already mentioned when discussing realization strategies, a variety of policy sciences roles should be located within policymaking organizations. Similarly, universities have important roles to fulfill in respect to policy sciences—both teaching and more theoretic and abstract research. But I think that policy research organizations, which can serve as a main framework for policy sciences research (and, to some extent, of teaching), should, in the main, be located neither within policymaking organizations nor within universities.

The reasons why policy sciences research is hard to locate within policy-making organizations are quite clear. The pressure of current problems, the propensity to satisfice, incremental change tendencies, practicality and prag-matism, the resistance to abstract thinking, and a variety of protective tendencies (such as postdecisional dissonance reduction, uncertainty avoid-ance, and ambiguity repression)—all these widespread features of organizations and organizational decisionmaking patterns combine to inhibit successful policy sciences research within organizations responsible for current policy-making. It is difficult enough to establish in such organizations policy analysis and minor policy sciences roles without imposing on them research functions, which are nearly completely inhibited by the above-mentioned features of organizational behavior.

Less obvious and, in many respects, more surprising to the uninitiated are the reasons which make universities a rather inhospitable environment for policy research organizations. These include, among others, the following: the tight compartmental structure, which inhibits interdisciplinary and even multidisciplinary endeavors; the distance from policymaking reality, which inhibits policy-relevant research; traditions of academic scholarship on the lines of the paradigms of normal sciences, which contradict the particular requirements of policy sciences and research; rules, patterns, and incentive structures for academic staff, which reward scientific conservatism and penalize innovation; tendencies to oscillate between olympic detachment from current issues and personal involvement of the "petition signing" type, both of which undermine possibilities for the particular contributions to better policymaking which characterize policy sciences research; and—more and more—the necessity to devote all one's time to teaching and, at the same time, inhibitive effects of mass student pressures on the intellectual detach-ment required for high-quality policy sciences research. Additional reasons may include the tradition of publication, habits of infighting, and internal politics, and more—but these are more minor reasons, which can be overcome successfully within the university environment. The seven main reasons mentioned above are harder to overcome and constitute, in the aggregate, a strong case against the location of policy research organizations at universities. I do not wish to imply that it is impossible to set up successful policy research organizations at universities; but, at the very least, this is a difficult assign-ment which should be attempted only when very favorable conditions exist.

My overall conclusion is that policy research organizations require locations outside policymaking structures, on one hand, and outside university structures, on the other hand. The preferable location varies between different countries, ranging from the nonprofit corporations in the United States, to government corporations with independent boards of directors or foundation-sponsored research institutes in a number of other countries. The concrete solution to the problems of organizations for policy sciences research will vary with the circumstances. But, whatever the preferable concrete solution may be, it must satisfy the various criteria mentioned above.

Having explored the organizational issues of policy sciences research at some length because of their critical importance for the future of policy sciences, I shall go on to some issues of research contents of policy sciences. I have already mentioned the two main clusters of policy sciences research—namely, research on policy sciences contents, such as policy analysis, mega-policies, metapolicies, and realization strategies, and inner-directed research on the methodologies, organizations, teaching, professionalization, and so on of policy sciences itself. I have also mentioned the dependencies of policy sciences research on close interaction with research on concrete policy issues. Rather than further to elaborate these general principles, I shall try to provide a view of the research tasks facing policy sciences through a short discussion of a sample of policy sciences research subjects, designed to provide an overview of the field:

1. Studies of the realities of actual policymaking is not one single subject, but rather a large and centrally important area for policy sciences research. Understanding the realities of policymaking, including the rules of change and the rules of ultrachange in respect to policymaking, is a central task for policy sciences, of critical importance for the understanding of policymaking, for identification of policymaking-influencing variables, and, ultimately, for policymaking improvement. This field of study also raises a whole spectrum of methodological issues on research designs and research tools of policy sciences, thus leading directly into some of the inner-directed research tasks of policy sciences. These deserve to be mentioned separately.

2. The development of research methods and research tools for policy sciences constitutes another important subject. The above-mentioned subject of study, namely, policymaking reality, exposes the need for novel research tools. Such research tools (each one of which constitutes, by itself, a subject for study and research) include, for instance, intensive case studies and methods for inductive generalization based on small numbers of intensive case studies; introspective explications of experiences by persons who fulfilled active roles in real-life policymaking; longitudinal research through partici-pant observation by real participants (that is, persons who fulfill real roles in policymaking but, at the same time, are willing to cooperate in studies of

policymaking—through keeping suitable diaries and using similar "current history" tools); comparative cross-national studies (e.g., a comparative study of policymaking on the cigarette-smoking issue is a good illustration, because of the identical nature of the problem and the manageable scope of the issue— which may, therefore, provide good insights into policymaking on the basis of contrasting the experiences of different countries); psychoanalytical studies of policymakers; backward reprocessing of information (i.e., restudy of available material, such as history, within a policy sciences framework); and so on.

3. To the methodologies of policy sciences, the study of instruments and tools to test the findings and recommendations of policy sciences should be added. These include, for instance, evaluation methodology, social experimentation, and comparative study as a substitute for experimentation.

4. In addition to an overall study of the policymaking system, and closely related to it, it is necessary to study policymaking and decisionmaking in the various components of the policymaking system. Research on decisionmaking and policymaking by individuals, by small groups, by organizations, and interorganizational clusters is an essential research subject for policy sciences.

5. Some features of policymaking reality are so important for policy sciences as to deserve special emphasis as a distinct research subject. These include, in particular, research on the impact of scientific advisors on policymaking and research on the impact of special policy analysis and policy research organizations on policymaking. For instance, research on the operations and impacts of the National Goals Research staff, the Presidential foreign policy advisor, and the Rand Corporation illustrates such particularly important (and, currently, very neglected and/or difficult to study) subjects in the United States.

6. Closely related to the already-mentioned subjects, but so important as to deserve specific emphasis, is research on the impact of different variables on policymaking, both in the aggregate and on the various components of the policymaking system, respectively. This includes studies on the impact of variables, such as information inputs; knowledge, personal characteristics, and biographic profiles of policymakers; organizational-structure features; and—to illustrate the more esoteric but not less important —the possible influence of various altered states of consciousness on policymaking behavior.

7. To pass on to a different cluster of subjects, I shall start with the need for intensive research—by appropriate methods, which are different from those of the behavorial sciences—on values which serve as goals for policymaking. Part of this research can be behavioral, aiming to find out what different publics want on different levels of awareness and what, in different

cultures, the main components are of "quality of life." However, parts of the value research (if we want to use the term *research,* but this does not really matter) will utilize methods leaning more on philosophy and law than on behavioral sciences. These methods include value morphologies, value taxonomies, examination of internal value consistency, examination of behavioral value compatibility and investigation of value competitiveness. Studies in psychology, welfare economics, and welfare theory on issues such as aggregation of values and units for value management, value consideration, and value comparison also belong to this subject.

8. Related to the issue of values, but distinct from it in many respects, is study on issue formulation and problem taxonomy. In part, this also has behavioral contents, such as the study of "agenda setting"—namely, what creates a "policy issue". Other components of this subject are issue morphologies, which permit cross-matrix examination of different issue formulations, so as better to pin down logical and behavioral overlappings, lacunas, and interdependencies. Lookout functions, directed at the early identification of emerging problems and issues, can also be regarded as belonging to this cluster of policy sciences research subjects.

9. The enumeration, classification, and elaboration of policy instruments constitute another very important subject for policy sciences, which deserves attention as a particularly interesting and neglected research subject. The idea here is to arrive at as exhaustive lists as possible of the different variables which can be used as policy instruments, and to study their domains of applicability in benefit-cost-risk terms, with as full explication as possible of underlying assumptions and boundary conditions. Every such list is provisional, because additional policy instruments can and should constantly be invented and discovered. Hopefully, the very process of systematic study of policy instruments as such will, among other benefits, provide a stimulus for the invention of new policy instruments. At the very least, comprehensive lists of policy instruments, with some guidelines on their usability under different conditions, may increase the range of alternative policy-instrument mixes that are considered in respect to concrete policy issues. The hope here is that policy instruments which usually are used for a limited number of problems may be found to be highly effective and efficient in respect to other types of problems where, traditionally, they never have been considered as an alternative. A good recent illustration is the idea of negative income tax as a substitute policy instrument for parts of the more conventional policy instruments used in social welfare.

The reader will have no difficulty in adding many further illustrations of policy sciences research subjects to the few provided here, ranging from social indicators to variables influencing policy-alternative creativity, from prediction methods to societal feedback designs, from experiences with planning to the impact of charismatic leaders on the styles of policymaking in different societies. This book includes many other subjects for policy sciences research; indeed, in many respects this whole book is composed of a set of subjects for policy sciences research. Therefore, I think that further discourse on policy sciences research here is unnecessary. My main conclusion is that policy sciences research is characterized both by unique organizational structures for engaging in such study and by particular configuration of subjects for research.

Recognition of the urgent need for policy sciences research, combined with recognition of the particular characteristics of policy sciences research, raises immediately the question, Who is to engage in such research? Parts of the answer to this query are supplied by the experience of policy research organizations which already exist and operate successfully. They do so, thanks to success in drawing, through self-selections and screening, suitable persons, who, given a favorable environment, slowly evolved the characteristics necessary for good policy sciences research. But progress at present is slow. Also, most policy research organizations tend to subsume policy sciences research under research on policy issues, in part, because of the background of the staff and pressures by clients. To overcome this weakness and to accelerate progress, a more rapid and concentrated preparation of policy scientists is needed. Especially attractive and promising is the idea of combining policy sciences research with training of policy scientists within a new type of policy sciences advanced teaching program. This brings us to the next subject of inquiry.

CHAPTER 14

Teaching of Policy Sciences

Teaching of policy sciences is needed on different levels and in different modes. In order to prepare the future citizen for his roles in public policy-making, some rudiments of policy sciences—in particular, policy analysis—should be included in the school curriculum. Certainly, college students should be exposed to policy sciences during undergraduate studies. Taking into account the growing amount of schooling provided to the population and the economic feasibility and even desirability of delaying entrance into the labor market, devoting one year of undergraduate studies to the study of social issues and ways to handle them—including parts of policy sciences—may constitute a desirable reform of university education, particularly in the United States. When we go up the academic level, policy sciences should constitute one of the main core subjects in all professional schools, the graduates of which in fact participate in policymaking, such as law, public health, physical planning, management, and social welfare. The more theory-oriented graduate schools—such as social sciences—should also give a massive dose of policy sciences, so as to prepare their graduates for more useful contributions to policymaking in various advisory and other roles. Not only during university studies should policy sciences be taught, but special courses for politicians, news commentators and reporters, senior executives, and similar policy-involved groups are an absolute necessity for increasing the contribution of policy sciences to the improvement of policymaking.

A detailed discussion of the problems of policy sciences teaching in all these frameworks is premature. Before policy sciences can become a wide-spread subject for teaching, it must first be further developed, both in the theory and in application. Therefore, I will focus my comments on the most advanced level of policy sciences teaching, the level at which the policy sciences scholars and policy sciences professionals must be educated and developed. It is this level, too, at which the teaching of policy sciences can and should be combined with research in policy sciences, and which, there-fore, constitutes an activity most critical for the advancement of policy sciences. My examination of the teaching of policy sciences as a policy sciences developmental activity focuses, consequently, on a doctorate pro-gram in policy sciences. With the help of this discussion of an advanced policy sciences program, the main problems of lower-level and shorter ver-sions of policy sciences teaching are also exposed and examined.

Policy research organizations may well be preferable locations for advanced policy sciences teaching. But, to be nearer to reality, I will construct a university doctorate program in policy sciences.[1] Within this framework I will comment also on the possibilities for advanced policy sciences teaching at policy research organizations.

The ideal university prototype program presented in this chapter is a doctorate program in policy sciences at regular universities, including two years' residency devoted to study and then the writing of a dissertation. (I am using the term *doctorate program* in its United States meaning. In many European and South American countries the equivalent would be a special postdoctorate degree or diploma. In some other European countries a new type of degree may be preferable to trying to fit the proposed program into the structure of contemporary degree requirements.)

Essential is the requirement to locate the program at the doctorate level. It is possible and often useful to have policy sciences programs, or some components of such a program, at other university levels, as already mentioned. But a doctorate level seems preferable, and even essential, for the following reasons:

1. The students already have a solid background in an established and well-developed discipline, thus (*a*) avoiding the dangers of superficiality associated with too early preoccupation with a yet underdeveloped supra-discipline, and (*b*) bringing to policy sciences necessary inputs from a variety of disciplines.

2. Hopefully, the students are still open-minded enough to absorb the novel paradigms of policy sciences, having avoided the strong trained-incapacity-reinforcement of many traditional doctorate programs.

3. It is one of the characteristics of policy sciences that learning and advancement of the state of knowledge must proceed hand in hand. Therefore —and especially at the present stage of underdevelopment of policy sciences— teaching, learning, research, and application must be integrated. This requires mature students of a type most probably recruitable at the doctorate level.

4. By making this a doctorate program, it is fitted, as far as possible, in the established academic and professional structure—making easier student recruitment, university approval of the program (under some circumstances), and absorption of the graduates of the program into academic and professional positions.

---

[1]This part leans heavily on my article, "Teaching of Policy Sciences: Design for a University Doctorate Program," *Social Sciences Information* 9, no. 2 (1970): 101–22.

For other views and descriptions of some policy sciences university programs, see two special issues of *Policy Sciences* devoted to "Universities and the Teaching of Policy Sciences," namely 1, no. 4 (1970) and 2, no. 1 (1971).

Let me now present some main features of the proposed program.

Objectives

One main objective of the proposed program is the preparation of researchers, scholars, and university teachers in policy sciences. But, in doing so, special attention must be paid to the specific desired characteristics of policy sciences academicians, particularly in respect to interaction with reality and policymaking actuality. Therefore, the preparation of policy sciences academicians can and should proceed together with the preparation of policy sciences professionals—close contact and, indeed, exchange between these two groups being one of the unique features of policy sciences.

Another main objective of the proposed program is to train professionals for serving in policy sciences positions in the public policymaking system. This includes, for instance, positions in systems analysis and program budgeting units, in planning units, in legislative staff units, and in the growing number of various types of policy research organizations.

I will return to the problems of policy sciences professionals in the next chapter. But one comment is necessary here: With recognition of policy sciences as a distinct profession and after demonstration of its usefulness for better policymaking, the creation and institutionalization of additional professional positions for policy sciences personnel in the policymaking system can be expected. Indeed, taking into consideration contemporary interests in the application of systematic knowledge and structured rationality to social problems, the expected demand for policy scientists is already greater than can reasonably be satisfied by new programs during the next few years without compromising their quality.[2]

To further clarify the nature of policy sciences teaching, let me emphasize that the objectives of a university program in policy sciences do not include the preparation and training of micro-"change agents." In contrast to the broad approach of policy scientists, which requires some detachment and a macroscopic view, micro-change agents operate largely through close personal involvement and emotional commitment in imminent and local situations. Certainly, micro-change agents should be familiar with the basics of policy sciences and able to appreciate their uses and limitations; also, both as an educational experience and perhaps for moral reasons, policy scientists

[2]This raises the important question of how to protect policy sciences from being ruined by becoming too much of a fashion (as is the case in some respects with "futuristics"), by serving as a haven for academic failures, or by being used as a flag of convenience by a number of low-quality "consultants." The establishment of carefully designed doctorate programs in policy sciences at reputable universities is a main way of reducing such risks by providing a reference group for recognition of high-quality academic and professional activities. But this reference group should not be exclusive, so as to permit the turmoil, search, and movement necessary for crystallization of new scientific paradigms and a new profession.

should spend some time of their career working as micro-change agents. But, in principle, these are different roles requiring separate university programs.

Students

In design, conception, and objectives, I think—frankly speaking—that a doctorate program in policy sciences should be an elite program directed at the top one percent of doctorate students—students who not only are able successfully to take a very tough and demanding program, but will enjoy it and thrive on it. Other programs should satisfy interests and requirements in policy sciences as an important part of a variety of academic and professional departments and schools. But a special doctorate program in policy sciences should be reserved for the best of the very good—in academic capabilities, in motivation, and in character. This is necessary because of the already-mentioned characteristics and difficulties of policy sciences and because of the breadth and depth of knowledge and of the capacities required for their development and study. A second reason for strictness in requirements would be the presumptuous appearance of a doctorate in policy sciences and the necessity to build up the credibility of such a hubris degree; therefore, only very top candidates should be admitted to such a program and graduated from it.

Not only should admission to a doctorate program in policy sciences be limited to top candidates from the point of view of personal qualifications and qualities, but some real-life experience should also be required. With individual exceptions, no one should continue from kindergarten to a doctorate in policy sciences without spending a few years on the way working in some institution, preferably a complex one, such as a community organization, something like the United States Peace Corps, an army, or some other public or political organization. I think the reasons for this requirement—in terms of maturity, experience, and tacit knowledge—are so obvious in respect to an advanced policy sciences program as not to require detailed elaboration. Let me just add that short internship programs during academic studies are no substitute for this requirement, being too artificial and too protected to serve as a useful surrogate for real work experience.

For reasons of group interaction, cross stimulation, and capacity for multiple teamwork, a minimum critical mass of students is required. My impression is that a group of less than fifteen students in each entering class may be below that minimum critical mass.

A group of fifteen entering students is also necessary to assure the desired diversity. No specific demands should be made in respect to the undergraduate and graduate background of the individual students. But in respect to each entering class of students, diversity in background should be sought. A mix including graduates in social sciences and economics, physical sciences, mathematics, law, engineering, and medicine is preferable in most respects, though the difficulties of achieving communication and the burden imposed on the teachers in such a group must be recognized.

In order to provide basic and shared background knowledge, all students must satisfy a number of academic requisites before starting the first year. Ways to make this a feasible requisite without impairing disciplinary diversity include (*a*) advance announcement of the requisites, so that interested students can try to meet them during their graduate studies, and (*b*) arrangement of special preparatory summer courses carefully designed to meet the requisites. (Acceptance into the program can be announced earlier, contingent on participation in summer courses needed to meet the entrance requisites.)

Minimum academic entrance requisites should include the following:

a. Mathematics, including some calculus, mathematical reasoning, and finite mathematics with emphasis on probability. The requirement here is for an understanding of mathematics and an ability to follow mathematics on the level of introduction to operations research and advanced economics.

b. An introduction to economics, including basic concepts in macro- and micro-economics and in welfare economics. Here, the main emphasis is mainly on an economic approach to resources allocation problems.

c. An introduction to research methods and statistics, with emphasis on the appreciation of main concepts and problems.

d. Some behavioral sciences. For those who had no behavioral sciences in their earlier studies, it will be necessary to design a special innovative course, directed at familiarizing the student with selected basic concepts and themes of behavioral sciences within a unified approach.

Ideally, minimum academic entrance requisites should also include these:

e. A second modern language, in which significant policy sciences relevant literature and material is available. This includes not only the main languages (French, German, Japanese, Russian, or Spanish) but also a number of European languages less widely used, in which a rich policy-relevant literature is available, such as Dutch or Swedish.

f. Some appreciation of physical and life sciences and engineering sciences. For those who had no physical and life sciences or engineering sciences in their earlier studies, it will be necessary to design a novel course—parallel to the one in behavioral sciences, but even more difficult to prepare—directed at familiarizing the student with selected basic concepts and themes of physical and life sciences and engineering sciences and their fundamental world view. A minimum requirement is that the students be able to comprehend the main developments of sciences and to understand most articles in publications such as *Penguin Science*

News and *Scientific American.*[3]

These additional requirements can in part be satisfied also during the first year of residence.

Student time and energy is the scarcest of all resources in so demanding a program as proposed. Therefore, students should be able to devote all their energies to their studies. This implies (*a*) adequate financial aid, adjusted to age and family situation, and (*b*) smooth administrative arrangements relieving the students of red tape and providing them with adequate facilities for studying (books, typing facilities, computer time, etc.).

Learning Dimensions: Contents, Curriculum, and Methods

The development of policy scientists on the doctorate level involves multidimensional experiences. In particular, as significant parts of policy sciences, such as policy analysis, involve more of an approach and skill than only detailed techniques, learning depends significantly on development of tacit knowledge, orientations, and patterns of perception and apperception. Similarly, requirements in respect to creativity, "human relations," and the ability to apply nomographic knowledge to ideographic situations need to be developed—again involving levels of personality and knowledge additional to explicit knowledge.

Therefore, a multiplicity of learning methods is required. These methods in addition to more traditional lectures, readings, exercises, colloquia, and seminars—have to include, as a minimum, gaming, cases and projects, internship, a new type of dissertations, and study tours. Also, some experimentation with personality development methods is indicated. But before discussing some problems of learning methods, we should explore some issues of contents and curriculum.

As a basic core, all students should develop significant knowledge in three areas of policy sciences, namely, (*a*) prescriptive policy theory and policy analysis tools, (*b*) decisionmaking and policymaking behavior, and (*c*) institutional change. The contents of these areas can be concretized in part as follows:

Area of Policy Sciences	Some Relevant Subjects
a. Prescriptive policy theory and policy analysis methods	Economics, benefit-cost analysis, systems analysis, operations research, strategic analysis, simulation techniques, mathematical models, policy analysis, planning theory, general systems theory
b. Decisionmaking and policymaking behavior	Organization theory, psychology of judgment, political behavior, public policymaking, science and government
c. Institutional change	Social change, theories of social development, organizational reform, attitude-changing techniques, institution building

[3] I am indebted to some of my physical and life sciences and engineering sciences colleagues at The Rand Corporation both for pointing out the need for this requirement and for reassuring me that such a course can be designed and successfully implemented.

Also, all students must be acquainted with basic relevant tools and instruments, including research methods and computers.

The necessity to develop new courses to meet these core needs must be emphasized. Some of the knowldege can be conveyed through standard courses, such as introduction to operations research, cost-benefit analysis, and psychology of judgment. But, in the main, new courses must be developed in careful coordination to assure coverage of main subjects without undue redundance. Thus, for instance, budgeting is relevant for all three core areas; social indicators can be included in the second area and/or in a tools and instrument course; evaluation should be emphasized within all areas; and social experimentation should be extensively treated in an innovative research method course.

All the core needs must be integrated in an overall policy sciences framework. In part, this integration is to be achieved by the special teaching methods, to be discussed below. But a number of new courses in policy sciences as such are required and constitute a central component of the core curriculum.

Every student should also select a specialization, to which he devotes about 25 percent of his time. This specialization can be in a method (such as operations research or systems and policy analysis) or in a policy issue area (such as education and manpower, strategy and foreign relations, health) or in a combination of methods and a policy issue area (such as physical planning, Research and Development, accelerated modernization problems).

Receiving a doctorate in policy sciences implies that the person is well equipped with knowledge and some experience in respect to policy-relevant approaches and methods. But my impression is that something more is implied—that a person having so high-sounding a degree has also at least some familiarity with main current problems in their historic perspective, both past and future. He should satisfy a demand which I would formulate as a slogan as follows: "To a doctoral candidate in policy sciences no significant human and social problem should be strange." What I have in mind here goes beyond having approaches, methods, and tools for significant penetration into different policy problems and having studied in depth some methods and/or issue areas. Some substantial knowledge on a broad range of main current problems, too, is needed.

To move in that direction, the following suggestions are offered:

a. In developing cases, projects, and similar teaching material, an effort should be made to use issues and illustrations dealing with a variety of problem areas.

b. A series of guest lecturers, workshops, and colloquia should deal with main current problem areas. For instance, one session a week might be devoted to an acute issue, with emphasis on learning basic relevant facts and designing a policy analysis network.

c. A seminar early in the program should be devoted to the time dimension of human and social problems, dealing, on one hand, with the significance of the past and ways to explore it, and, on the other hand, with the methods and perspectives of futures studies. Later on, in the workshops, case studies, etc., care should be taken to examine the importance of the time dimension and work out the relevant past origins and futures contexts.

d. Care should be taken not to neglect foreign and military problems.

e. There is need for some action to provide students who have no substantive work experience in other types of societies with a broad, cross-cultural perspective. A well-organized extensive study tour to a very different country may be helpful.

Another main problem is one of values. I have in mind here not the methodological issues of treating values in analysis but the educational issue: how to help becoming policy scientists to crystallize their personal substantive values. There is no universally valid suggestion in this matter; much depends on finding inspirational teachers who can help the students in value exploration, perhaps within a student-managed framework.

Exposing the students to vicarious experiences of human suffering and misery may also be essential—not through an internship in an "aid-giving" organization, but by sharing for some time the day-to-day life of some "miserables." In different conditions various activities are helpful; but let me reemphasize the need to make an intense effort to sensitize students to humanity, which stands above and beyond the concepts and tools of policy sciences.

Relatively easier (though still very difficult) to prepare for—through case studies, for instance—are the role conflicts of the policy scientist and the tensions between his contradicting values as an individual, as a scientist, as a citizen, as a policy advisor, and as a member of some organization.

As already indicated, curriculum cannot be discussed in isolation from teaching methods and material. I have previously mentioned the need for using a variety of teaching methods. This desideratum will be easily agreed to. The trouble is that preparation of suitable teaching material and suitable guidance and supervision of advanced teaching methods are so important and—at the same time—so difficult, time-consuming, and expensive that a very concerned effort is required, with a special staff. Indeed, preparation of teaching material may be a task for a cooperative endeavor of interested universities and may require close symbiosis with suitable policy research organizations.

The ideas of new teaching methods and the difficulties of their realization can be illustrated by a short exploration of three of them:

a. Workshops in applied policy analysis. In these workshops, students (as individuals and in differently combined teams) deal with real—or at least realistic—policy issues and policy projects. Without doubt, this is a most important component of a policy sciences program, critical for integration of knowledge, for developing capacities to apply knowledge to concrete policy problems, and for conveying tacit knowledge and skills. I think about 25 percent of student time should be devoted to such workshops. For success in achieving these goals, close involvement of the senior faculty in the workshops is required. Also required is much effort to prepare suitable cases and projects for workshop teaching, structured in a series designed to achieve efficient learning experience by proceeding from the simple to the complex, from the quantitative to the qualitative, and from low-level to high-level problems. Also, the material should be designed to illustrate the special characteristics of different policy issue areas and the uses of different tools and techniques. (Preparation of such material too may be suitable for a cooperative endeavor between a number of universities and, even more so, may require close cooperation between universities and policy research organizations).

b. Internship programs in policy analysis. An essential component of teaching policy analysis is learning through applied work on real problems as members in high-quality teams. The best—and, at present, the only—places for doing so are the policy research organizations. Therefore, arrangements should be made to permit students in the policy sciences program to do at least two summer internships in one of those organizations.

c. New types of dissertation. The form of the doctorate thesis should be adjusted to the special characteristics of the proposed program: dissertations on policy sciences research subjects are desirable, but the dominant dissertation type should be an applied study of a policy, megapolicy, or metapolicy issue with alternative improvement recommendations. Arrangements are needed to permit writing of such dissertations while working on teams in policy research organizations, the dissertation dealing with the individual work of the candidate being supplemented by reports on his contributions to the team study. (This requires again close cooperation and symbiosis between university policy sciences programs and policy research organizations.)

Faculty

The innovative nature of the proposed program constitutes a great challenge to the faculty and imposes on it a significant burden, as it is up to the faculty to build up a new discipline while teaching it. Strong commitment to the idea of policy sciences is therefore essential.

The faculty must be interdisciplinary in origin, including members from the various behaviorial sciences, economics, and management sciences. Planning, law, life sciences, and systems engineering also have important contributions to make. Early involvement by a historian, a philosopher, and a depth psychologist are important to avoid some of the omissions shared by most contemporary behavioral sciences, decision sciences, and planning disciplines.

The faculty should also be rich in applied experience. It is essential to have on the faculty some members with extensive experience in applied analysis, preferably in a senior professional position in a high-quality policy research organization. Also needed are faculty members with high-level experience in public organizations and politics.

The required diversity of the faculty in policy sciences further aggravates a problem made difficult by the youth of policy sciences—namely, to what extent the policy sciences program should have a full-time faculty of its own and/or share teachers with other, already-established departments. A well-known difficulty with faculty members shared between a new interdisciplinary endeavor and a well-established discipline and department is the tendency of such faculty members to orient themselves mainly to their well-established discipline and department. As a result, their innovative contributions to the interdisciplinary endeavor are minimized and the program is reduced to a multidisciplinary one. Therefore, a distinct faculty in policy sciences is required. This faculty should be large enough to include the main relevant disciplines, to teach the basic core courses, and, in particular, to prepare and supervise the workshops. Tentatively, it seems that a minimum viable number for such a faculty—which, with suitable assistance, also administers the program—is about ten to fifteen faculty members. These full-time policy sciences faculty members can and should be supplemented with faculty shared with other departments and with some part-time faculty from among professionals working in policy research organizations, planning units, and the like.

Recognizing the danger of becoming more utopian than ideal, I shall try to set down the main specifications which should be met in the aggregate by the faculty (in no order of priority). Some of these specifications require more than one person; several others can be satisfied by one and the same person, while some should be shared by all faculty members. But all of them should be aimed at while building up a policy sciences faculty:

a. Inventive capacities in respect to social problems, including wild ideas on new designs for living, new forms of culture, etc.

b. A good knowledge of history, with special attention to social history, combined with an interest in applying history to problem solution. Especially necessary is good familiarity with social history.

c. Intensive work in ethics and the philosophy of values, both analytically oriented and applicative.

d. Integrative knowledge in the behavorial sciences, combining a broad view of them, good knowledge in them, and an interest in their application to social problems.

e. Good familiarity with the physical sciences and life sciences, with special interest in technological forecasting, in science-created social problems, and in the human implications of scientific discovery.

f. Intensive work in depth psychology, in the broad sense of the term, and special interests in applying a depth-psychological frame of appreciation to social problems and human issues.

g. Broad expertise in strategic theory and strategic analysis, with special interest in the application of the methodology of strategy analysis in different problem areas.

h. Close familiarity with the internal political scenery and with the local society in general, with a good sense for both "the art of the possible" and for possibilities to make the improbable feasible.

i. Good cross-cultural and cross-societal knowledge, including living experience in a number of different countries, combined with an interest in bringing to bear the cross-society knowledge and experience on social problems – both by providing a broad perspective and by specific comparison.

j. Personal close familiarity with main social problem areas, based on applied work in those areas—but without having lost a broad perspective.

k. A broad general systems approach with special interest in its prescriptive implications.

l. Expertise in management sciences and their techniques.

m. Intensive knowledge in economics, with special emphasis on microeconomics, welfare economics, and modern political economics.

n. Knowledge of organization theory and change theory in general, with special emphasis on the dynamics of change and the role of change agents.

o. A policy sciences approach, in the broad sense of that term.

As already admitted, this looks like a dream list. But I do think one can move in its direction by careful selection of faculty members and by a long-range development policy. The latter involves hiring young faculty members and helping them to move in the needed directions and encouraging the best students to prepare themselves for future work as pioneers of policy sciences research and teaching.

The internal dynamics of the policy sciences faculty—part-time and especially full-time—raises some complex issues because of the innovative nature of the program, its experimental nature, and the need for much dynamic change and learning through trial and error. In such a new program, faculty members cannot stand aloof from one another, with each one enjoying a monopoly on a defined segment of the program, which no colleague can criticize. Indeed, close interaction, mutual learning, and creative conflict are required. It seems, therefore, that two acceptable patterns of faculty dynamics are either (*a*)frank peer-group interaction on the basis of equality or (*b*) a senior faculty head and a group of highly capable, more junior faculty members, who accept the guidance of the faculty head. Difficult for the development of a program in policy sciences is a faculty composed of a set of *stars,* all equally senior, self-confident, unwilling to permit others to interfere with *their* subjects, and uninterested in what their colleagues are doing.

The continuous development of the policy sciences faculty poses some additional requirements, including maintenance of close contact with policy realities and development of knowledge through applied policy analysis, redesign of policymaking units, social experimentation, and similar policy advisory and policymaking-improvement activities. In order to enable and encourage policy sciences faculty members to engage in such activities, arrangements should be worked out permitting frequent leaves of absence to work in policy research organizations and encouraging consultative activities while at the university. At the same time, some restraints may be necessary to assure priority for research and teaching and to protect the development of policy sciences. The adjustment of faculty advancement criteria to take into account the quality of applied work which cannot be published in full is also necessary.

Faculty-Student Relations

The high quality of desired students combines with the dynamic nature of the program and some of its features in shaping the preferable extent of student participation in the faculty roles of developing the program and managing it. Ignoring exogenous variables specific to different countries and universities, from the point of view of the policy sciences program it seems that students have at least two important roles: (*a*) student reaction to the program and their subjective feelings of achievement and learning constitute one of the secondary criteria for evaluating the program, and (*b*) some parts of the program might preferably be managed by the students (for instance, value exploration, as mentioned above).

When efforts to engage in personality development are included in the program—or as a result of general university climate and/or policy—students may tend to form a community and may be willing to assume additional responsibilities in respect to guidance of the program as a whole. While many will regard this in principle as a desirable trend, nevertheless I would like to point out some possible dangers, which require that the faculty maintain adequate control:

a. The tough demands of the proposed policy sciences program will generate frustrations and even hostilities, which may motivate students to try to soften the program.

b. The essentially intellectual, somewhat clinical, and policy-oriented approach of policy sciences may result in adverse reactions, especially during their first year, by students who may prefer action to the policy sciences approach and who may therefore try to move the program into micro-change-agent directions.

Students will realize at a more advanced stage of their studies both the necessity for tough demands and the potential special contributions of policy sciences to social well-being and humanistic values. But the faculty must maintain sufficient control over the program to bring the students to the more advanced stages. Therefore, student participation should be encouraged and student influence welcomed, but without being permitted to determine the basic features and orientations of the program.

Relations between University Programs and Policy Research Organizations

I have already mentioned several times the need for close relationships between university teaching of policy sciences and policy sciences organizations—in respect to preparation of teaching material, student internships, and staff exchanges. The necessary interdependence is even deeper and closer because of the nature of research in policy sciences, which involves application of policy sciences to real problems and issues and which therefore takes place optimally in special policy research organizations.

The dependence is mutual: on one hand, policy research organizations are a main locus for policy sciences research, but, on the other hand, teaching activities and involvement with high-quality doctorate students are very healthy for policy research organizations—by advancing conceptual and methodological explication and systematization, by forcing reexamination of implied assumptions and tacit theories, and by providing agitation and some heresy. Therefore, the already-mentioned desirability of symbiotic relations between university policy sciences programs and policy research organizations is apparent.

This symbiosis can take place on the basis of three main structural arrangements:

a. Establishment of a policy research operation at the university as part of the policy sciences program or, at least, in very close relationship with it.

b. Establishment of policy sciences teaching programs at policy research organizations.

c. Establishment of close ties and intense cooperation between structurally separate university programs and policy research organizations.

Establishment of a policy research organization at the involved university looks like a good idea. But, upon closer examination, the picture becomes less attractive, for the reasons explored in chapter 13. To those reasons, the danger must be added that the desire to assure high-quality research and arrive at supportable alternative recommendations may transfer attention from student training to applied policy research, with increasing reliance for the significant work on faculty and consultants and displacement of students into routine jobs. (This applies less to large and already well-established policy research organizations, which add students to their research activities.)

Some variation of establishing a policy research organization at the university may, nevertheless, be convenient and preferable in different countries. Thus, in some countries, a policy research organization may optimally be sponsored by the government and located within a university, maintaining close symbiosis with a policy sciences teaching and study program which is completely a university operation. But one response to the problem which requires much caution is that a university set up a policy research institute composed of one or two full-time staff members and dependent on part-time university faculty and students for doing the real work. Such an institute is quite different in operations and products from an interdisciplinary well-sized and fully equipped policy research organization and cannot achieve the diversity, depth, and broadness of policy research of the latter.

The best justification for nevertheless setting up a small university policy research institute, under some conditions, is that no adequate policy research organizations are available, and that starting with a small policy research institute may sometimes be a good way to build up a full-scale policy research organization. This, for instance, may well be the case in a number of modernization countries.

Very attractive, as already mentioned, is the idea of establishing policy sciences teaching programs at policy research organizations. This depends, first of all, on the existence of such highly developed organizations—a condition met at present only in the United States.

When set up at a policy research organization, a policy sciences teaching program will emphasize instruction through supervised participation in on-going policy research work and teaching through individual tutorship. Also, the program will be more strongly oriented toward the preparation of high-quality professional policy analysts, rather than policy sciences scholars, teachers, and researchers. Therefore, university policy science doctorate programs and doctorate programs in policy sciences at policy research organizations are not identical, fulfill somewhat different needs, and are both useful and needed in countries where sufficient resources are available for maintaining a multiplicity of policy sciences programs.

The third possibility, of symbiosis between structurally separate university policy sciences programs and policy research organizations, is in many respects not only very effective but also highly efficient—by reducing the costs of far-reaching innovation and the risks of failure. When well-estab-lished policy research organizations do exist, the building up of cooperative relationships with them in respect to development of teaching material, student internship, staff exchanges, etc., is—as already mentioned—both essential and preferably from the point of view of the universities. It is also often preferable from the point of view of the policy research organizations, though the latter should sometimes also try to set up a policy teaching pro-gram of their own.

A number of different combinations may fit various countries. Thus, sometimes simultaneous development of a government-related policy research organization (not at the university) and of a university policy sciences teach-ing and study program—with close relations and some personal overlap between these two—may be preferable. The possible variations are many, but in one way or another the necessity of backing up a university policy sciences teaching and study program with a policy research unit must be met. This is essential for the supply of inputs and teaching opportunities needed for successful doctorate-level teaching of policy sciences, and indeed for the advancement of policy sciences as a whole.

External Requirements and Activities

A doctorate program in policy sciences, as proposed in this chapter, is a difficult endeavor, being not only innovative and experimental but having a high probability of meeting skepticism from many of the traditional disci-plines' faculty, and derision from many of the "self-made" policy practi-tioners. Therefore, much external support for the program is essential. Two main forms of essential external support for a program in policy sciences are as follows:

a. Strong support by top-level university academicians and university administration. Not only is such support needed in order to establish a doctorate policy sciences program on the lines proposed in this chapter, but maintained high-level intense support is essential -for continuous development of the program.

  b. Liberal financial support in the form of grants (by foundations, government agencies, business, etc.) which are both long term enough to provide time for development through experimentation (i.e., for at least five years) and elastic enough to meet changing needs and unconventional types of expenses (e.g., student study tours, as suggested above).

Also needed, as already indicated, are mutual support and cooperation among various policy sciences university programs and between them and policy research organizations. Such cooperation should preferably be international in scope,[4] so as to provide policy sciences teaching with a broad perspective and advance the role of policy sciences as an important contributor to better public policymaking in different countries.

This leads me to my last point, namely, the external roles of the proposed university doctorate programs in policy sciences: such programs should serve as one of the main developers of new scientific paradigms, which hold much promise for the uses of systematic knowledge, structured rationality, and organized creativity in the service of humanity. Therefore, such programs are not only pioneers of science, but also bear a heavy long-range social responsibility. Such programs should, as a result, serve as centers of activity for the advancement of the utilization of policy sciences as a main novel resource for better societal and human conscious self-direction, in addition to advancing policy sciences as a new academic supra-discipline.

A main feature of any policy sciences program must be a capacity for learning and change. The novelty of policy sciences and its teaching requires, on the behalf of its proponents, teachers, and professionals, a constant eagerness to learn and improve, on the basis of experience and contemplation, research and teaching alike. A program in policy sciences should therefore evolve through sequential decisionmaking, trying to maximize learning by

[4]International cooperation is especially important for the modernizing nations, for which establishment of regional policy sciences teaching programs may be both a very good and the only feasible alternative. International cooperation should not be limited to policy sciences teaching, but should also cover policy research organizations. Thus, international cooperation may overcome the shocking (though not surprising) fact that in the whole world there is not even one interdisciplinary and critical-mass-achieving policy research organization devoted to the problems of comprehensive development policies.
Also attractive is the idea of policy sciences teaching at a World University, perhaps in cooperation with a Global Policy Research Organization.

the staff as well as the students. But recognition of the need to revise the program and to view its first years as a work-bench experiment does not make superfluous careful preparation and thought in advance. In other words, even though provisional, the initial design of a doctorate program in policy sciences should be based on the best available knowledge, ideas, and experiences. This requires intense cooperation and exchange of views between those interested in policy sciences and its teaching.

Teaching of policy sciences is closely tied in with the preparation of policy sciences professionals. Consideration of the latter will, therefore, shed some additional light on the teaching of policy sciences, too.

CHAPTER 15

Professionalization of Policy Sciences

Examination of the doctorate program in policy sciences already provided some insight into the profession of policy scientists, as I perceive it. Many questions concerning policy sciences, as a profession cannot usefully be discussed at the present stage, being essentially open issues to be resolved through learning and experimentation. For instance, the question of whether one should speak about one unified "policy sciences profession" or whether one should rather consider a broad range of policy sciences professionals, who share a common core of policy sciences, but tend to specialize in particular policy areas or in clusters of methodologies—this is a question, consideration of which is premature. Nevertheless, the conception of policy sciences professionals is so crucial for the design of policy sciences as to require at least some provisional treatment. What I would like to do, therefore, is to consider some main features of the policy sciences profession; I am trying to pick out those features which are more important and critical and which, at the same time, are less sensitive to the many uncertainties surrounding the future development of policy sciences and policy sciences professionals.

On the basis of my conception of policy sciences and on the basis of available experience with the various precursors of policy sciences professionals, it seems that the following comments on the professionalization of policy sciences are supportable, at least as tentative observations which can serve to sensitize use to the main relevant issues:

1. Policy sciences is, in part, a profession, in addition to being a scholarly endeavor and a research activity. Perhaps another name, such as policy analyst, should be used for policy scientists occupying professional positions in policymaking units. It is also possible, as already indicated, that the policy sciences profession includes a cluster of subspecializations and suboccupations. But the professional nature of large parts of policy sciences must be emphasized.

2. Rotation between professional and other policy sciences activities is desirable. Close interconnections between more theoretic and more applied activities are one of the characteristics of policy sciences. Therefore, it is desirable for most policy scientists to move back and forth between different policy sciences roles, including teaching and more theoretic research, policy research in special policy research organizations, and policy sciences staff positions within policymaking units. Rotation between more professional and

more research and teaching-oriented activities is, therefore, an important characteristic of the policy sciences profession.

3. The just mentioned rotation requirements are a part of necessary developmental career patterns, but the latter must include more than rotation between different policy sciences activities. The broad requirement, "No human and social problem is a stranger to the policy scientist," and the serious dangers of tunnel vision and narrowness of mind impose a heavy burden on professional policy sciences career patterns, which must be designed to assure continuous growth and development. Frequent refresher opportunities through courses and workshops; periodic sabbatical leaves of absence for extended periods to permit advanced learning combined with contemplation; and broad rotation, including movement between a variety of organizations and roles that are characterized by different perspectives—these are among the required means for the continuous development of policy sciences professionals. To this, I think, one should add the need for mind-enlarging experiences, including, for instance, periods of work in other cultures, and perhaps, even some developmental psychoanalysis. To fulfill in a responsible way the functions of improvement of policymaking and to avoid the dangers of becoming narrow technicians, unconventional career patterns to assure the continuous development and maturation of policy sciences professionals are necessary.

4. To achieve necessary mutual reinforcement, to build up suitable career patterns, and to reinforce moral constraints, professional organization is necessary. It is insufficient to train individual policy sciences professionals and then let them loose, each one by himself. Once policy scientists receive specific training at universities, the problem of professional identification will become easier and the establishment of professional organizations will not be hindered by the problem of entrance qualifications. Until then, and also later on, care must be taken to avoid the overrigidity of exclusive formal qualifications. But establishment of a professional organization of policy scientists is a necessary step for crystallization and advancement of the profession. This association should include all policy scientists, whether they happen to work in a more professional or in a more research-and teaching-oriented role. Exchange of experience, stimulation of academic and research activities, and encouragement of information flows—these are among the more conventional activities in which a policy sciences professional association should engage. Other necessary activities include, for instance, promotion of recognition of policy sciences as a profession, support for establishment of policy sciences advisory positions in various governmental and other policymaking organizations, educational activities designed to familiarize the public with the idea of policy sciences, assurance of availability of policy sciences advice

to various organizations and groups that are too small to build up a policy sciences staff of their own, and more.

5. A main requirement for the desirable development of policy sciences is a code of ethics for its professionals. Illusions should be avoided: drafting a code of ethics and even trying to enforce it in part through peer pressures is no guarantee that policy sciences—as all knowledge—will not be used for the worst in some instances. But a code of ethics can be of significant help in guiding the development of policy sciences on desirable moral lines and can aid the various categories of policy sciences professionals to handle the many difficult value dilemmas and ethical issues which they are sure to face. The principles of a code of ethics for policy scientists should include, among others, the following:

a. A policy scientist should not work for a client whose goals and values, in the opinion of the policy scientist, contradict basic values of democracy and human rights.

b. When the goals and values of a particular client contradict basic beliefs of the policy scientist, the policy scientist should resign rather than help in the realization of goals and values with which he intensely and fundamentally disagrees.

c. The purpose of policy sciences is to help in better policymaking, and not to displace legitimate policymakers and decisionmakers with policy scientists who become "gray eminences." Therefore, policy scientists shall try to preserve and increase the choice opportunities for their clientele, e.g. by always presenting a number of alternatives. In particular, a policy scientist should not hide an alternative because it contradicts his own personal values and preferences.

d. Policy scientists should explicate assumptions and should present clear value sensitivity analyses, so as further to increase the judgment opportunities for their clientele.

e. A policy scientist should refuse to prepare studies, the sole purpose of which is to provide a supporting brief to an alternative already finally decide upon for other reasons and considerations by his client.

f. Policy scientists should not work for clients who do not provide necessary access to information and opportunities for presentation of studies and their findings.

g. All forms of conflict of interest should be avoided, including utilization of information for private purposes and presentation of recommendations in respect to subject matters in which a policy scientist has a personal and private interest.

The idea of policy sciences is a new one. Even more novel is the conception of policy sciences professionals who specialize in the contribution of systematic knowledge, structured rationality, and organized creativity to the improvement of policymaking. The policy sciences professionals constitute a main bridge between policy sciences as an academic study and policy sciences as an imminent factor for the improvement of real policymaking. Therefore, building up policy sciences professionals, institutionalizing them, and constantly advancing their capacities and qualifications are main conditions for the success of policy sciences in its missions and, at the same time, constitute a main result of a successful policy sciences endeavor.

PART V

Implications
of Policy Sciences

By now it is quite clear that even partial success in the building up of policy sciences on the line proposed in this book will have fargoing implications for various social institutions and, I think, for the future of humanity as we now know it. This being a book on the design of policy sciences, and not on the longer-range futures of humanity, I will limit my comments on the broader implications of policy sciences to a few remarks in the epilogue. More properly a subject matter of this book are the direct implications of policy sciences for the two most closely related institutions, namely, politics and science.

CHAPTER 16

Implications for Politics

Frankly speaking, policy sciences is directed at the reform of politics—if not all of politics, then at least a very significant part of it. Directly, policy sciences is concerned with only one aspect of politics, through a very important one, namely, policymaking. Nevertheless, any significant success by policy sciences in influencing policymaking will also have fargoing repercussions for the whole of political culture and institutions, including such basic facets of politics as elections, consensus maintenance, and interest articulation. Contemporary political science well recognizes that even seemingly technical and managerial tools, such as planning-programing-budgeting systems, have important impacts on the power distribution and, therefore, are basically political in nature. *A fortiori,* policy sciences, which is explicitly oriented toward redesign and even novadesign of the policymaking system, does have fargoing implications for politics. These implications go beyond a narrow conception of "scientific advice to politics," which assumes that the main political institutions are fixed, and are not themselves subjected to redesign. While policy sciences does not interfere with the basic tenets of democracy (or of any other political ideology or regime, with the exception of a purely mystical or "führer"-oriented one, which is unable to accept the strong rationality assumptions of policy sciences), nevertheless, the ideas of policy sciences and their realization carry with them many implications for politics.

Some of these implications, which reach beyond specific points to political culture as a whole, can best be presented metaphorically in the context of the familiar fairy tale, "The Emperor's New Clothes." The young child, it will be recalled, was the only one to dare to cry out, "The Emperor is naked!" Not only is policy sciences (i.e., its scholars and professionals and their research findings) expected to cry out loudly, "The Emperor is naked!" but the same emperor is expected to pay policy sciences to observe him closely; should give policy sciences a medal for breaking up a pleasant myth; should invite policy sciences to go with him to the bathroom so as to have full opportunities to examine the king during his most intimate hours; and should institutionalize policy sciences so as to make sure he cannot change his mind on policy sciences later on, after he gets tired of being exposed as undressed and after possibly some revolutionary movement uses his exposure by policy sciences to gain support and plan a conspiracy. Furthermore, not only should policy sciences be asked to declare that the emperor is naked, but it should be asked

123

both to design a choice of clothes for him and to suggest the tailor. However picturesque, this metaphor does bring out the fundamental tensions between policy sciences and contemporary politics, the difficulties of asking politics to support and accept policy sciences, and the innovations in political culture necessary in order to permit improvement of policymaking in accord with policy sciences.

It is the subject matters and contents of policy sciences which make it so important for politics and, at the same time, so hard to accept by politics. Policy sciences does not limit itself to providing information which politicians are expected and demanded to take into account. Policy sciences goes much further: it presumes to tell politicians not only what to take into account but how to make up their minds. In other words, policy sciences not only provides inputs for the political decisionmaking processes but wants to reshape and reform the political decisionmaking processes themselves. Thus, policy sciences transgresses into what is regarded as the "secret art" of politics, thereby endangering the self-image of politicians. Policy analysis presumes to tell politicians how to consider policy issues; megapolicies provide new dimensions which politicians are required to confront when considering policies; even further reaching are metapolicies, which explicitly want to redesign and sometimes novadesign the policymaking system, including its political components; added to all this are realization strategies, which frankly proclaim that policy sciences is not neutral about its own role in policymaking. All this imposes a great deal on the relations between policy sciences and politics, between *nova scientia et potentia*.

Let me move on from these general remarks to four more specific comments on the implications for politics of policy sciences:

1. A main implication of policy sciences for politics is that many tacit assumptions and implicit choices are made explicit. Thus, goals of policies, underlying assumptions on the future, tacit megapolicy judgments, and patterns of handling uncertainty are all made explicit and are transformed from something to be worked out indirectly and rather unconsciously into explicit and quite clear-cut choice issues.

The posing of explicated and clear-cut choices fits well the democratic creed, because it increases the actual control exercised by politicians over politics. But it fits neither the contemporary features of politics nor some essential requirements of politics.

The softening of disagreements and the avoidance of politically and individually hard choices, through nonformulation of explicit alternatives and avoidance of explication of underlying assumptions and values—these are features of contemporary politics in all countries, which are both convenient and, to some extent, necessary. These features are convenient, because they avoid the hard work, internal conflicts, external collisions, and intellectual requirements associated with clear confrontation of choices within a framework of explicated assumptions and goals. They are, to some extent, essential, because maintenance of basic consensus and of essential coalitions which permit cooperation between different parties and diverse points of view depends on some repression and ignorance of alternatives. Maintenance of basic consensus and of essential coalitions depends even more so on leaving many basic assumptions and underlying values unexplicated, so that ambiguity and simultaneous preference for contradictory values and assumptions can serve to meet the requirements of consensus, agreement, and coalition maintenance. Thus, convenience and necessity combine to make incremental change, or agreement on abstract and nonoperational values only, and usually both of them in combination—a very preferable mode of policymaking, especially on politically loaded issues.

Frank recognition of the factors inhibiting explication of values and of assumptions and hindering consideration of clear-cut alternatives is essential for the understanding of policymaking reality and for its improvement. Because of the essential functions fulfilled by ambiguity and nonexplication, an optimal situation must include a lot of ambiguity and unexplanation; that is, under optimal conditions—given the basic characteristics of human beings in their political behavior as known to us from prehistory until now—the uses of policy sciences for better policymaking are not unlimited. Therefore, it is incorrect to state in an unrestricted way that "the more policy sciences is used—the better it always is." Let me again try to illuminate this point with a simple metaphor. Policy sciences theory states that one should not leave the problem of crossing a river until the river is reached; rather, one should survey the territory in advance, identify rivers flowing through it, decide whether it is at all necessary to cross the river—and if so, where and how to cross it—then prepare in advance the materials for crossing the river, and design a logistic network, so that the material is ready when the river is reached. But practical politics will often say that not only should the problem of crossing the river be left until the river is reached, but one should leave it until one is already up to the throat in water—when imminent danger will result in complete agreement that the river must be crossed at once and in the recruitment of energy to do whatever is necessary to get through the river alive. By leaving consideration of the problem of crossing the river up until the last moment, so a partly correct claim may go, one is at least sure of reaching the river, rather than being bogged down through premature controversy on how to cross the river and on whether one should not stop moving so as to avoid the problem of the river altogether.

This metaphor, however simple, is relevant to our problem. In particular, the usefulness of sometimes not using policy sciences and related rationality methods should be emphasized as a counterbalance to the tendency of some self-styled policy scientists (and many of their precursors, such as planners, economists, physical scientists, and so on) to ignore the essential features of politics—features which not only are unavoidable but are often necessary to permit human progress. Particularly reprehensible and unjustified is the tendency to look down on politicians forgetting that it is often much harder to become a high-level politician than to become a tenured professor: the competition is much tougher and screening mechanisms are much harder to pass. Politicians are highly qualified professionals in their own right, possessing a great deal of tacit knowledge from which policy sciences has—as already pointed out—a lot to learn.

While the positive functions of some of the policy sciences contradicting features of contemporary politics should be explicitly recognized, nevertheless, it seems that reality errs a great deal in the direction of repressing alternatives, reducing explication, and overrelying on tacit processes. In other words, examination of the realities of policymaking leads, I think, to the clear conclusion that preferization of policymaking requires much more explication of values and assumptions and much more consideration of clear-cut alternatives than is at present the case. My conclusion here is, therefore, that politics must be redesigned so as to be able to handle clear-cut alternatives, clarified values, and explicated assumptions much more than is presently the case. But this conclusion is somewhat tempered by my recognition that there is no linear positive correlation between better policymaking, on one hand, and more value and assumption explication with posing of clear alternatives, on the other hand. From a certain point on, the latter may endanger essential features of politics. The fact that we are far off from the point of diminishing utility of additional value and assumption explication and clear alternative formulation is no reason to ignore the existence of a point of diminishing utility and even of negative utility. This is of practical importance, because in respect to individual policy issues and some particular social circumstances, that point may be nearer than many policy scientists might like to think. Even more important for preserving a correct perspective of politics and its needs from policy sciences is bearing in mind the limits of usefulness of value and assumption explication and of clear alternative formulation.

2. One clear requirement in respect to politics resulting from the development of policy sciences is for politicians to be better qualified in a number of respects. Without reducing in any way the tough demands on preferable politicians in respect to moral standings, representative stance, bargaining skills, leadership capacities, and so on, additional intellectual and emotional capacities must be added to the requirements from politicians. These additional requirements include the intellectual knowledge to understand and utilize policy sciences and the emotional capacities to handle and use policy sciences. On the intellectual level, these requirements include knowledge of the funda-

mentals of policy sciences, with particular attention to the ability to absorb critically policy sciences studies and to appreciate both the domains of usefulness and the domains of uselessness of policy sciences. On the emotional level, requirements include capacities of handling the more disturbing and security-reducing aspects of policy sciences, such as uncertainty, explication of value contradictions, critical reexamination of favored tacit theories, and so on.

Requirements in respect to emotional capabilities are harder to meet than in respect to intellectual capabilities, though the latter also are not easy. Substantive approximation of the requirements may be impossible until the bases from which politicians are recruited are changed, through inclusion of relevant educational activities in all schools. Nevertheless, within the canons of democracy, which make the public the judge of who should become a successful politician, with everyone being entitled to serve as a candidate, a lot can be done to increase the qualifications of politicians. Feasible instruments to move in that direction include special courses for politicians after they are elected, ranging from a few study weeks to three or four months; arrangements for sabbatical leave for politicians to be spent in appropriate studies; and introduction of suitable courses into locations and schools from which future politicians are often recruited—such as law schools in the United States. I have already mentioned these ideas as possible metapolicy recommendations. Here, they serve to illustrate one type of essential implication of the development of policy sciences for politics. The necessity to improve qualifications of politicians, so they can handle policy sciences inputs and so they can fruitfully interact with policy sciences professionals, is all the more urgent because otherwise they will tend to ignore policy sciences or overrely on it and then counteract to it. However unconventional in terms of contemporary practice and however ignored in present behavioral sciences (including political science, which should know better), the need to improve the qualifications of politicians is a main implication of policy sciences for politics.

3. The development of policy sciences puts into sharp focus a fundamental issue of democracy, namely, the growing gap between increasingly difficult issues and increasingly complex policy-relevant knowledge, and the static capacities of citizens to understand these issues and form intelligent opinions on them with the help of the new knowledge. While based on a larger context, this dilemma is put into stark relief through the development of policy sciences. Policy sciences provides knowledge, concepts, and ideas of much significance for better policymaking. But unless citizens at large can understand this knowledge, at least in its rudiments, and utilize critically new findings so as to improve their role in respect to policymaking, then either the knowledge and findings remain unused or the division of influence be-

tween citizens and other components of the public policymaking system shifts further toward the latter, with even less influence for the citizen. Here we run into what I call aphoristically the third Dror law, which reads as follows:

> Unless the capacity of citizens to comprehend complex policy issues and to consider critically policy studies increases significantly—the role of citizens in shaping policies will either diminish or result in worse policies.

One of the main impacts of the development of policy sciences on politics is, therefore, to emphasize and reinforce the necessity to increase capacities of citizens to comprehend policy issues and improve their contributions to policymaking. At the same time, one of the main impacts of policy sciences on politics is that policy sciences can, in principle, supply an important means for improving the role of citizens in perferable policymaking—if policy sciences is suitably used.

One requirement for the utilization of policy sciences so as to improve the contributions of citizens to preferable policymaking is the production of policy sciences studies on acute and future policy issues for the public at large; I will deal with this requirement in the next point. Here I want to mention another requisite for the utilization of policy sciences so as to increase the contribution of citizens to preferable policymaking—namely, providing citizens with the capacities necessary to comprehend complex policy issues and to adopt positions in respect to them, which are both autonomous and of high quality. This involves conveying to the citizen knowledge in the basics of policy sciences and, even more important, providing the citizen with the basic frames of appreciation of policy sciences as a framework for building up his own opinions and positions in respect to policy issues.

This requires a whole network of educational activities, for adults as well as for future citizens while they are still in school. New tools, such as policy games and individual policy exploration programs, must serve as new means for adult education in policy sciences for better participation in policymaking. In respect to schools, both new tools and new ways of teaching traditional subject matters (such as mathematics and history) are required. Whatever the technical instruments for providing citizens with qualifications in the elements of policy sciences may be, the very need to equip citizens with a capacity to utilize policy sciences in a basic form and the need for citizens to be able to consider on their own policy sciences research findings—these are among the most important political implications of the advancement of policy sciences.

4. The need for redundancy in policy sciences research and in policy

sciences-based research organizations and the necessity to disperse them throughout the societal direction system have already been mentioned several times. Therefore, this does not require much additional elaboration. Let me just repeat that—in order to preserve pluralism, in order to reduce the risks of misuse and underlying biases in policy sciences, and in order to increase at the same time the impact of policy sciences on actual policymaking—diffuse distribution of a large number of different forms of policy sciences-based policy research organization and of other forms of policy sciences research activities is essential. Particularly necessary also are arrangements to provide policy sciences aid to non-governmental and non-establishment groups so as to assure maximum aggregative contribution to better pluralistic policymaking by combining the specific contributions of policy sciences with a large variety of opinions, values, assumptions, and interests. It goes without saying that policy sciences should be utilized by all the different components of the public policymaking system, legislators not less than executives, courts not less than planning units, parties not less than offices of presidents and prime ministers.

Very interesting is the problem of assuring policy sciences research for the public at large. Quite a number of countries have auditor generals or comptroller generals who report to the public on honesty and efficiency in the governmental administration. In many countries public commissions, royal commissions, task forces, and similar *ad hoc* arrangements provide the public from time to time with high-quality studies of policy issues—though, usually, in a form hard for the average citizen to absorb with his present equipment. Some countries, such as Sweden, are quite systematic in presenting before the public various pros and cons of proposed policies, with various degrees of issues. But with the development of policy sciences, much more is needed: what is required are some policy sciences-based policy research organizations which prepare studies for the public at large on policy issues, both short-range and long-range ones. These studies have to be thorough and penetrating; but the findings have to be presented in forms and languages that are easily communicated to the public and that are designed to increase opportunities for autonomous position-taking, rather than the selling of one solution or another. Studies by such policy research organizations, which are working for the public at large, should be widely distributed through various media of communication, including written studies, presentation on television, and so on.

Interesting to ponder is the possibility of providing constitutional protection to policy sciences research on policy issues for the public at large. Whether this and similar proposals and possibilities will be realizable in the future or not, the implications of policy sciences for the role of citizens in policymaking and on the need to improve the capabilities of citizens to avail themselves of policy sciences for better policymaking are among the more important ones of the development of policy sciences for politics.

Interfaces between policy sciences and politics constitute a main leitmotiv of this book as a whole. Therefore, I think the four points discussed in this chapter are sufficient to bring out the nature of the implications of policy sciences for politics. In particular, they serve to bring out six main duties which politics must accept in regard to policy sciences: to understand, to maintain, to inform, to listen, to consider, and to respond—but not necessarily to accept. There are many other impacts, but just as important as identification of what the implications of policy sciences for politics are is clear recognition of the many essential features of politics to which policy sciences has little to contribute. Leadership, vision, ideologies, social prophecy, consensus maintenance, distribution of power—these are some of the main functions of politics which are quite insensitive to the development of policy sciences in the foreseeable future. The magic of politics, its excitement, and its imaginative functions as a master architectonic art—these, too, transcend the functions of policy sciences and its impact on politics.

Policy sciences is concerned with one main issue of government and politics, which is a very important one, but not the only important one and probably not the single most important one—namely the relationship between power and knowledge. With the advent and progress of policy sciences as a new type of knowledge which is very salient for policymaking, a new symbiotic relationship between that knowledge and power must be built up. This, in turn, implies significant transformations in politics. But these transformations are far short of a real metamorphosis of the basic values and institutions of politics, which may or may not be necessary, but is not directly related to the advancement of policy sciences.

CHAPTER 17

Implications for Science

Many readers of this book will readily agree that politics must change so as to adjust itself to progress in knowledge and to avail itself of the contributions of policy sciences. These very readers—who will, in the main, belong to the science community—may be less disposed to embrace some of the implications of policy sciences for science and the science community. Therefore, these implications deserve all the more attention and emphasis.

The whole of this book deals with the necessity to change parts of science so as better to fit the needs of policymaking improvement. Weaknesses of contemporary normal sciences, needs for new scientific paradigms, requirements for new forms of policy research organizations to advance policy sciences and apply them, proposals for new training programs for policy scientists, and suggestions for a novel policy sciences profession—all these are, simultaneously, requisites for the development of policy sciences and implications of policy sciences for science and the science community. Repeating these and similar points would be negatively redundant. Instead, let me sum up these recommendations and findings and supplement them with a few additional comments in a somewhat different form, so as to provide a sharp view of at least some implications of policy sciences for sciences.

The main implications of policy sciences for science and the science community can be summed up under four main points:

1. A first implication of policy sciences for science is that the science community should give support to policy sciences and encourage the required innovations in paradigms, research, teaching, and professionalization.

However simple sounding, this is a very hard-to-realize implication. The barriers to policy sciences innovations in the science community are discussed in chapter 6. It is sufficient, therefore, to refer here again to that earlier discussion. Since chapter 6, the many innovative aspects of policy sciences, which involve fargoing changes in respect to the fundamental characteristics and features of science and its structure, have been clarified. Therefore, an unavoidable conclusion is that the various barriers to fundamental innovation and, in particular, to innovations in the organization of scientific activities and scientific structures operate very intensively in respect to policy sciences.

The conservative tendencies of the science community and the resistance to fundamental innovations are reinforced by the organizational conservatism of science and research organizations. Universities will not be too happy with educational and teaching activities that may preferably take place at policy research organizations; departments will not be too happy with new teaching and research frameworks that crosscut their traditional division of the world; and university administrations will be quite disturbed by competition from new types of institutions for limited funds. The strong pressures exerted nowadays on the science community and its organizations by students, the government, and the public at large may, on one hand, somewhat increase the propensity to innovate; but, at the same time, they may lead to much entrenchment, which hinders experimentation and readiness to engage in risk-taking innovation.

The case should not be overstated. After all, most of the proponents and pioneers of policy sciences do come from the science community, even if they have atypical careers. If science has much inbuilt conservatism, it also has strong inbuilt dynamics for change. Therefore, I believe the necessary support for policy sciences from the science community will come forth. But the strength of the forces operating against policy sciences in the science community must be recognized. The overcoming of those forces and the recruitment of strong support for policy sciences are among the main implications of policy sciences for science and the science community.

2. The barrier to support for policy sciences in the science community are compounded by the main implication of policy sciences, which involves the substantive contributions of science to policymaking. This main implication is a strict demand for self-discipline on behalf of the science community in dealing with policy issues. At the very same time that more and more scientists have serious misgivings about science contributions to the welfare of humanity; at the very same time, that many scientists share a cultural value crisis and doubt many of the goals and assumptions which they tended to take for granted; and at the very same time that the science community is under strong attack by students, on one hand, and many politicians, on the other hand—at this very same time policy sciences adds a heavy constraint on the reaction of scientists to all those pressures, by requiring a strict discipline in study and pronouncements by scientists (as scientists) on policy issues.

This self-restraint requirement, which constitutes a main impact of policy sciences on science, relates to the widespread weaknesses of science contributions to policy, as discussed in Part I and especially in chapter 1. Mix-ups between reliable facts, assumptions on doubtful facts, substantive values, different megapolicies, and issues that belong to the area of competence of a variety of disciplines—these and similar weaknesses of contemporary science contributions to policymaking are unacceptable at present.

With the development of policy sciences, they become completely reprehensible. This implies that every scientist who wants to make a science contribution to policymaking must do so within an explicated policy analysis network, which will serve to clearly indicate the different components of his contribution and their respective validity, bases, and features. As already indicated, this implication does not imply any restraint on creativity, innovation, and imagination. But it requires from science contributions to policymaking to be very self-conscious and very self-sophisticated in reflecting on one's own contribution to policymaking with the help of methodologies, concepts, and frameworks provided by policy sciences. The necessity to re-examine science contributions to policy with the help of policy sciences formats does impose a heavy burden on such contributions, one which is radically different from the present propensity of scientists to be quite freewheeling in presuming to make science contributions to policymaking.

This implication of policy sciences for science takes an even more aggravated form when its concomitant requirement to distinguish quite sharply between policy contributions by scientists as such and participation in policymaking by scientists as human beings and citizens is considered. This is so important an implication as to deserve separate consideration.

3. The third implication of policy sciences for science, which is closely related to the second one, is the need for quite clear-cut differentiation between the contributions of science via scientists to policymaking and the participation of scientists as citizens in policymaking. This differentiation is not based on any illusionary belief in the possibilities to distinguish completely between facts and values or to arrive at a really value-free science. The interdependence between facts and values, and the dependency of the scientific endeavor on values in respect to selection of issues, identification of variables, and interpretation of findings—all of these must be fully recognized. Nevertheless, there is a great deal of difference between recognizing the unavoidability of some mix between the contributions of science and the contributions of the persons who happen to engage in science, and giving up attempts to distinguish as much as possible between those two.

The advent and advancement of policy sciences sharpen the distinction between science contributions to policymaking and between scientists who try to influence policies in specific directions which they regard as desirable. This distinction exists even if there is in the latter case some influence of scientific knowledge on value preferencs and much use of scientific knowledge in preparing briefs to advance the policy directions which one favors. Modern tendencies for policy involvement by scientists make it all the more necessary to try to sharpen this distinction. Advocacy roles, predictions of ecological doom, attempts at social prophecy—all these are important social functions in which scientists, as persons, can fulfill important roles. But there is a radical difference between those activities and the preparation of policy sciences studies, which permit the policymakers whom one regards as legitimate (whoever they may be, from the establishment to the general assembly of members of a counterestablishment group) to make their own decision on the basis of the best available aid by science. Even more un-scientific an activity are some forms of petition signing, in which case scien-tists try to use their reputation as scientists to support uncritically one policy or another, usually one on which they have no special expertise and often one which they have not tried to study with the help of the scientific approach they so ardently embrace in respect to their scholastic activities.

Let me be completely clear: nothing said here is intended to restrict and restrain political activities by scientists, ranging all the way from petition signing to becoming a candidate for the top political positions of one's coun-try. But I regard it as harmful, both to democracy and to the building up of science contributions to policymaking, to mix up personal political activities by a scientist or a group of scientists, with the application of scientific knowl-edge to policy issues. The distinction is not an easy one to make, but a maximum effort to push this distinction as far as possible should be made. Policy sciences will be helpful in providing a number of methods and tools for doing so. But policy sciences also pushes the need to try to distinguish as much as possible between science contributions to policymaking and the involvement of scientists as individuals in policy issues. Without such a distinction, the claim that policy sciences—and many components of normal sciences—can make an important contribution to policy improvement in a way which enhances rather than reduces the choice by legitimate policy-makers, and thereby the realization of democracy, may be doomed. As a moral duty, as a pragmatic necessity for the advancement of policy sciences, and as a requisite for the improvement of policymaking with the help of science contributions, a maximum effort is necessary to distinguish between science contributions to policymaking and individual participation by scien-tists as citizens in policymaking. To underline this need and to provide some means to achieve it in part—these are some of the implications of policy sciences for science and the science community.

4. The fourth, and I think the most important, implication of policy sciences for science is reassertment of the critical role of science for better policymaking, and for human affairs in general.

The role of policy sciences as a strong reassertment of the importance of science contributions for humanity is all the more significant in view of some present disenchantment with science and the appearance of some signs even of antiscientism, both in the public at large, in specific groups, and—however surprising this may sound—in the science community itself. Policy sciences combines recognition of its limited domain of applicability—and awareness of the broader but still limited domain of validity of sciences as a whole— with a strong claim that it, and science as a whole, can make most important contributions to humanity by improving societal capacities for conscious self-direction and self-transformation. It is this reassertment of the importance of science for human progress, combined with a demand for changes in science so as to be able to fulfill its potential role in human advancement, which constitutes the most important impact of policy sciences for science and the science community.

Epilogue
Some Open Issues of Policy Sciences

This book is aimed at providing a preliminary design for policy sciences. Viewing policy sciences as a possible new response by higher mental human capacities to the challenges of shaping human destiny, I have presented policy sciences as an attempt to improve policymaking through systematic knowledge, structured rationality, and organized creativity. With focus on the application of a scientific orientation to the improvement of public policymaking, policy sciences emerged as a new intellectual structure based on novel paradigms. With unique paradigms serving as its basis, policy sciences is distinguished by a particular set of main dimensions which cluster around the main issues of policymaking, namely, policy analysis, megapolicy, metapolicy, and realization strategy. To build up policy sciences, suitable research, teaching, and professionalization are required. When policy sciences does reach a higher level of development, it can be expected to have significant social implications, of which I explored, in particular, those for politics and for science.

This design left many questions open. That is all right, as the main purpose of the present book is not to write a history of policy sciences, and not even to write a prehistory of policy sciences, but rather to provide an additional stimulus to the development of policy sciences and to try to provide some help for taking the first steps on the way to building up policy sciences. But there are two issues that must not be left unmentioned, even though I cannot solve them. These are (1) the moral issue involved in the proposal to build up policy sciences, and (2) the question, What is the appropriate level of aspiration for policy sciences?

I have already discussed some secondary moral issues, namely, the compatibility between policy sciences and democracy and the necessity for a code of ethics for policy sciences professionals. More difficult and much more critical is the primary moral issue posed by the very mission of policy sciences, namely, to contribute to the improvement of public policymaking. Even when policy sciences is viewed as a passive factor, available for better policymaking when desired, the issue of misuse by bad policymakers of policy sciences so as more effectively to achieve their bad goals is serious. My statement that policy sciences ought to assume an active role and my proposition to regard realization strategies as an integral dimension of a preferable policy sciences design further aggravate this issue, by emphasizing the active role of policy sciences as a change factor in respect to policymaking.

The fundamental moral issue is posed by my claim that policy sciences is aimed at the improvement of policymaking, in the sense of contribution to

137

the making of policies which achieve more of goals determined by the legitimate policymakers after suitable value analysis, but—in the final analysis —determined by someone else, and not by the policy scientist as policy scientist. As noted by some of the critics of the notion of policy sciences, policy sciences is designed to provide a stronger engine and more capable navigational aids, but the direction in which to move is, at least in part, outside the concern of policy sciences, as such. Therefore, policy sciences can be misused for bad purposes, so as to realize more effectively and more efficiently undesirable and even horrible goals.

I think this danger is a real one. As all scientific knowledge, so policy sciences can be used for better and for worse. Medicine can be used to conquer disease or to produce biological weapons; weather control can be used to enrich humanity or to make desert production a mode of terrible warfare; genetic engineering can be useful for producing *homo superior* or for breeding totally obedient robotlike soldiers; and so on. I am willing to go a step further; on the basis of bitter experience, I assume that sooner or later every knowledge will also be used for the worse, though hopefully in a minority of cases.

To approach this problem, a distinction must be drawn between the moral responsibility of individual policy scientists, and of policy scientists as a community, and the very contents of policy sciences. In respect to the contents of policy sciences, concrete findings and detailed recommendations will vary with the underlying values accepted by policy scientists and dominant in their culture. Thus, within a democracy society, terror, mind control, and single-party leadership will be excluded from the domain of policy and metapolicy alternatives. But the basic orientations and methods of policy sciences are value neutral (within their explicated metaphysical assumptions), and a policy scientist in a totalitarian police state will have little difficulty— if he wants to do so, as probably some will—in adjusting the overall principles of policy sciences to his particular values and making recommendations abhorrent to his colleagues in other, democratic countries. This clear dilemma of policy sciences is shared with other disciplines: should we stop to develop knowledge which can be used for better or for worse—that is, practically all knowledge? Or should we further advance knowledge, trying to combine it with safeguards against misuse through much attention to the moral characteristics of the scientist, hoping that, all in all, progress of knowledge will be more for the better than for the worse?

My own choice is clearly for the second approach, namely, to advance knowledge, combined with efforts to increase the probabilities for its use for what I regard as the better. This general preference of mine, which is based on certain metaphysical beliefs on the nature of mankind and its destiny, is strongly reinforced in respect to policy sciences by the belief that, in the absence of policy sciences mankind is more in danger than with the presence of policy sciences, even if the latter is sometimes used for the worse. In other words, I think that presently available and emerging technology permits grievous harm to humanity through bad policies. Bad policies are quite probable for a number of reasons, which we have already explained. Therefore, unless policymaking is significantly improved, the probabilities of catastrophe are quite high. I believe that policy sciences is essential to reduce the risks of catastrophe while, at the same time, policy sciences, even if sometimes misused, will—in the worst case—add little to the longer-range risks to humanity. Therefore, I do think that the overall expectation in respect to the impact of policy sciences on human fate is, in the balance, on the positive side. My conclusion is that while the risks of policy sciences being misused for the worse should be explicitly recognized, nevertheless, those risks are worth taking because of the potential much more significant contributions of policy sciences for the better.

Accepting my basically optimistic assumptions that, after all and in the longer run, policy sciences—and sciences as a whole—will be used more for the better than for the worse, the second issue which I would like to take up concerns the appropriate level of aspiration for policy sciences. Assuming that policy sciences indeed succeeds in the sense of a suitable body of knowledge being built up and somewhat used, what difference can this be expected to make in human and social affairs?

Let me start with the more fundamental issue, namely: Can policy sciences be expected to have any influence on human destiny, in the longer run? In many respects, I tend to answer this question in the negative. Human destiny, in the main, is shaped by forces and factors beyond our understanding and beyond our intervention, over which even highly developed policy sciences cannot be expected to have much influence (unless some radical discontinuity in our understanding of social phenomena occurs).

But some exceptions must be made to this generalization. These exceptions make policy sciences critical, not only for the shorter-range issues of societal direction, but for the basic destiny of humanity. I am referring to the awesome possibility that human decisions may be capable of reshaping the human species itself. Whether this feat is achieved through influencing the genetic code, through mind-amplifying drugs, or through man-computer tie-ins, the supreme test for policymaking capacities will surely be posed by any such ability to reshape Homo sapiens itself. In respect to this possibility, the quality of policymaking may well determine the fate of humanity, and, therefore, the capabilities of policy sciences significantly to improve policymaking may assume determinative importance.

Also of significant and perhaps crucial importance for human destiny is the avoidance of irreparable damage to the human species. Total nuclear poisoning and the possibility of upsetting the basic thermal balance of the earth—these are two illustrations of possibly irreversible consequences for the human species of bad policymaking. The avoidance of such a consequence is a main policy goal, for the achievement of which policy sciences may be critical or, at least, highly important.

If we leave aside these extreme cases—each one of which, by itself, fully justifies intense efforts to develop policy sciences—the increasing capacities of humanity to shape the environment, society, and human beings make absolutely necessary improved policymaking capabilities. One of the main purposes and missions of policy sciences is, therefore, to break out of what I aphoristically call the Second Dror Law:[1]

While human capacities to shape their environment, society, and human beings are rapidly increasing, policymaking capabilities to use those capacities remain the same.

In order to realize novel policy problems which cannot be solved by contemporary policymaking capabilities, it is sufficient to think about the possibilities of influencing the gender of the child during conception—something that, by all predictions, will soon be feasible with simple chemical means. Please note that here we speak about a probable misbalance between males and females, that is, a breakdown of one of the fundamental characteristics of humanity and, indeed, of all forms of life. How to prevent such a breakdown and control its consequences poses unprecedented policy issues. Should one try to prohibit the use of gender-determining chemicals altogether? And what if this chemical is easily synthesized, so that control is ineffective? Should one allocate quotas through a randomizer? Or in accordance to some genetic preferences? And what about a possible neighboring country which encourages a ratio of ten men to one woman so as to prepare itself for conquering the world? However science-fiction-like this and similar questions seem to be, they are the stuff of which future policy issues are made. Weather control—another hard problem for policymaking—may be farther off in the future. But presetting the gender of children may become feasible in the near future. We are totally unprepared for such clearly foreseeable policy issues (there seems to be not even one single policy research group in the whole world systematically thinking on such issues). Furthermore, our policymaking system is unequipped to handle such issues. The expectation that policy sciences may make some contributions to the capabilities of policymaking systems to handle such issues—even if we leave aside the more

[1]The First Dror Law is discussed in Yehezkel Dror, *Ventures in Policy Sciences* (New York: American Elsevier, 1971)

extreme cases of reshaping Homo sapiens or endangering its existence—is, again, by itself, a sufficient justification for maximum efforts to advance policy sciences.

Leaving aside policy issues of the future and abnegating a longer time perspective in respect to human destiny, we are left with the ordinary policy problems of the contemporary world. And these are sufficient to keep us awake all night, wondering about our inabilities to handle what are, by now, the routine problems of policy. Misery, poverty, war, the gap between the haves and have-nots (individuals and countries alike), the utilization of limited space for increasing humanity, environmental issues, human and community relations, distribution of health services, individual and public safety, recreation, transportation, telecommunication, and so on and so forth—these are among the areas and issues for policymaking, all and each one of which are filled with difficult problems that, at present, we are quite incapable of handling. Even if we adopt a minimum level of aspiration in respect to the contribution of policy sciences to these issues, the expected significance of such a contribution justifies again intense efforts to develop policy sciences. The avoidance of some bad policies and the improvement of overall policymaking by, say, 10 percent (I am using this quantitative number as a qualitative concept)—such minor ambitions already constitute a break with the tradition of human policymaking, which has not really improved from the early prehistory of humanity until quite recently, and, perhaps, even until now.

The more one learns about the realities of policymaking, the more one tends to despair of human capacities to direct humanity. The more I observe higher-level policymaking in a variety of countries and situations (admittedly, my observations are sporadic and not based on any representative sampling), the more my impression is that a housewife who studies *Consumer Reports* before going to do her shopping is relatively much more prudent than many senior policymakers before making important decisions. Paradoxically, it is exactly those weaknesses of contemporary policymaking which hold forth great promises for the future, if an effort is made to improve policymaking.

If the present qualities of policymaking reflected a high level of effort to improve policymaking, then, indeed, there would be little hope for the future. Once a system exhausts much of its potential, further improvement is very difficult and soon becomes practically impossible. But when a system operates at a level very much below its capacities, then, if suitable steps are taken, its qualities of operation may advance by a step-level function and improve by jumps. This, I think and hope, is the situation in respect to the policy-making system, redesigned and novadesigned as may be necessary.

The very absence of policy sciences today constitutes an important chance and opportunity to try to significantly improve policymaking through introducing policy sciences as a new element. At the least, policy sciences will somewhat improve policymaking; perhaps it may also serve as a catalyst for changes in other policymaking-shaping forces and combine with them to bring about a radical transformation of the qualities of policymaking. But even if we adopt a low level of aspiration and even if we say that the chances of success in achieving those aspirations of policy sciences are less than .1—even then the pay-offs of success are so tremendous and the consequences of failure so catastrophic as to make the effort to develop policy sciences not only cost-effective but a moral duty.

Bibliography

This list includes a number of selected books, usually recent ones, as a guide to some of the policy sciences relevant literature for the interested reader. A more comprehensive literature survey up till 1967 is provided in the Bibliographic Essay, Appendix D of my book *Public Policymaking Re-examined* (San Francisco: Chandler, 1968), pp. 327–356.

Even though first published twenty years ago, still very important is, of course, Daniel Lerner and Harold D. Lasswell, ed., *The Policy Sciences: Recent Developments in Scope and Method* (Stanford: Stanford University Press, 1951; 4th printing, 1968). This early view of policy sciences should be contrasted with the most recent treatment of policy sciences by the inventor of that concept, namely Harold D. Lasswell, *Pre-View of Policy Sciences* (New York: American Elsevier, 1971).

A broad selection of policy sciences items appears in the new periodical *Policy Sciences,* published by American Elsevier, the first issue of which appeared in Spring 1970. A different integrated discussion of a variety of policy sciences concepts and applications is presented in Yehezkel Dror, *Ventures in Policy Sciences* (New York: American Elsevier, 1971).

Still worth reading as presenting the basic challenge which policy sciences tries to face is Walter B. Pitkin, *A Short Introduction to the History of Human Stupidity* (New York: Simon and Schuster, 1932). The basic concept of "scientific revolution"—which is highly relevant to the idea of policy sciences—is presented in Thomas S. Kuhn, *The Structure of Scientific Revolutions* (Chicago: University of Chicago Press, 1962). Applicability of this concept to social science is examined in Robert W. Friedricks, *A Sociology of Sociology* (New York: The Free Press, 1970). A broad relevant perspective is provided by Alvin W. Goulder, *The Coming Crisis of Western Sociology* (New York: Basic Books, 1970), and—in a different way—by Theodore J. Lowi, *The End of Liberalism: Ideology, Policy, and the Crisis of Public Authority* (New York: W. W. Norton, 1969).

During the last few years, some progress has taken place in respect to the empiric study of some aspects of policymaking, especially in the United States. A good reader which reflects this trend, is Ira Sharkansky, ed., *Policy Analysis in Political Science* (Chicago: Markhan, 1970), which also includes a good bibliographic list. Another representative reader is Edward V. Schneider, ed., *Policy-Making in American Government* (New York: Basic Books, 1969). Good illustrations of quantitative approaches to the study of policymaking are, for instance, Thomas Dye, *Politics, Economics and the Public: Policy Outcomes in the American States*

(Chicago: Rand McNally, 1966) and Ira Sharkansky, *The Politics of Taxing and Spending* (Indianapolis: Bobbs Merrill, 1969). A more traditional but not less useful approach is used in James L. Sundquist, *Politics and Policy: The Eisenhower, Kennedy and Johnson Years* (Washington, D.C.: The Brookings Institution, 1968). More monographic is Francine F. Rabinovitz, *City Politics and Planning* (New York: Atherton Press, 1969). Historic and, I think, fascinating, is R. G. Tugwell, *The Brains Trust* (New York: The Viking Press, 1968). A good case study is Robert L. Crain, Elihu Katz and Donald B. Rosenthal, *The Politics of Community Conflict: The Fluoridation Decision* (Indianapolis: Bobbs Merrill, 1969).

A broad and comprehensive policy approach is proposed in Amitai Etzioni, *The Active Society: A Theory of Societal and Political Processes* (New York: The Free Press, 1968). Unique as a policy-oriented textbook in political science is Joyce M. Mitchell and William C. Mitchell, *Political Analysis and Public Policy* (Chicago: Rand McNally, 1969). A short introduction to a policy approach is provided by Charles E. Lindblom, *The Policy-Making Process* (Englewood Cliffs, N.J.: Prentice Hall, 1968). Good collections which present diverse approaches well illustrating the increase of interest in policy studies, are Raymond A. Bauer and Kenneth Gergen, ed., *The Study of Policy Formation* (New York: The Free Press, 1968), and Austin Ranney, ed., *Political Science and Public Policy* (Chicago: Markham, 1968). A good reader is Fremont J. Lyden, George A. Shipman and Morton Kroll, eds., *Policies, Decisions and Organizations* (New York: Appleton-Century-Crofts, 1969). An additional good treatment is, for instance, Francis E. Rourke, *Bureaucracy, Politics, and Public Policy* (Boston, Mass.: Little, Brown and Company, 1969). Also interesting are Michael C. Reagan, *The Administration of Public Policy* (Glenview, Ill.: Scott, Foresman, 1969) and Ira Sharkansky, *Public Administration: Policy-Making in Government Agencies* (Chicago: Markham,1970).

Broad normative frameworks for policy sciences are provided in Stafford Beer, *Decision and Control: The Meaning of Operational Research and Management Cybernetics* (London, John Wiley, 1966); Yehezkel Dror, *Public Policymaking Re-examined* (San Francisco: Chandler, 1968); and—from a different point of view—Charles E. Lindblom, *The Intelligence of Democracy* (New York: The Free Press, 1965). Fascinating in its normative approach is also Warren F. Ilchman and Norman Thomas Uphoff, *The Political Economy of Change* (Berkeley: University of California Press, 1969). A different basis for a new supradiscipline comparable in some respects to the idea of policy sciences is presented in Constantinos A. Doxiadis, *EKISTICS: An Introduction to the Science of Human Settlements* (New York: Oxford University Press, 1968). For exploring further the potentials of design theory as a basis for policy sciences, see Gary T. Moore, ed., *Emerging Methods in Environmental Design and Planning* (Cambridge, Mass.: M.I.T. Press, 1970).

Broad perspectives on some of the problems to be faced by policy sciences are provided, inter alia, in Rene Dubos, *Reason Awake: Science for Man* (New York: Columbia University Press, 1970); in Aurelio Peccei, *The Chasm Ahead* (Toronto: Macmillan, 1969); and in Geoffrey Vickers, *Freedom in a Rocking Boat: Changing Values in an Unstable Society* (London: Allen Lane, Penguin Press, 1970). Very stimulating are also some of the essays in Erich Jantsch, ed., *Perspectives of Planning* (Paris: OECD, 1969).

To pass on to some of the foundations of policy sciences, significant progress has taken place in many of them during the more recent years. Particularly relevant is the progress made in decisions theory, in systems analysis, in applied social sciences, and in futures studies.

Good introductions to recent work in decisions theory are Howard Raiffa, *Decision Analysis: Introductory Lectures on Choices under Uncertainty* (Reading, Mass.: Addison-Wesley, 1968) and D. J. White, *Decision Theory* (Chicago: Aldine, 1969). A good recent introduction to uses of operations research is Harvey M. Wagner, *Principles of Operations Research: With Applications to Managerial Decisions* (Englewood Cliffs, N.J.: Prentice Hall, 1969). More technical progress is illustrated, for instance, by D. G. Champernowne, *Uncertainty and Estimation in Economics* (San Francisco: Holden-Day, Vol. 1, 1969, Vol. 2, 1970, Vol. 3, 1970) and by Erik Johnsen, *Studies in Multiobjective Decision Models* (New York: Barnes & Noble, 1969). Highly interesting and relevant are M. M. Botvinnits, *Computers, Chess and Long-Range Planning* (New York: Springer, 1970); John P. Crecine, *Governmental Problem-Solving: A Computer Simulation of Municipal Budgeting* (Chicago: Rand McNally, 1969); and J. K. Friend and W. N. Jessop, *Local Government and Strategic Choice: An Operational Research Approach to the Processes of Public Planning* (Beverly Hills, Calif. Sage Publications, 1969).

Very important for policy sciences is recent progress in systems analysis. The two best introductions to the subject are E. S. Quade and W. I. Boucher, eds., *Systems Analysis and Policy Planning: Applications in Defense* (New York: American Elsevier, 1968) and C. West Churchman, *The Systems Approach* (New York: Delacorte Press, 1968). More technical, but highly important, is Gene H. Fisher, *Cost Considerations in Systems Analysis* (New York: American Elsevier, 1971). Additional discussion and some illustrations are provided by Stephen Enke, ed. *Defense Management* (Englewood Cliffs, N.J.: Prentice Hall, 1967) and by David B. Bobrow, ed., *Weapons System Decisions: Political and Psychological Perspectives on Continental Defense* (New York: Praeger, 1969). Problems of applicability to non-military issues receive increasing attention, but so far without too much results. Some of the involved problems are discussed in Guy Black, *The Application of Systems Analysis to Government Operations* (New York: Praeger, 1968) and Harold A. Hovey, *The Planning-Programming-Budgeting Approach to Government Decision-Making* (New York: Praeger, 1968). Also relevant are Robert L. Chatrand, Kenneth Janda and Michael Hugo (eds.), *Information Sup-*

port, Program Budgeting, and the Congress (New York: Spartan Books, 1968) and Harley H. Hinrichs and Graeme M. Taylor, *Program Budgeting and Benefit-Cost Analysis* (Pacific Palisades, Calif.: Goodyear, 1969). More technical and engineering-oriented is Bernard H. Rudwick, *Systems Analysis for Effective Planning* (New York: John Wiley, 1969).

An increasing number of policy analyses of various issues gets published. Markham Publishing Company, for instance, has a special Series in Public Policy Analysis, with Julius Margolis and Aaron Wildavsky as editors. Different approaches can be illustrated by four books, out of many: Frank W. Banghart, *Educational Systems Analysis* (New York: Macmillan, 1969); Anthony Downs, *Urban Problems and Prospects* (Chicago: Markham, 1970); Yehezkel Dror, *Crazy States: A Counterconventional Strategic Issue* (Lexington, Mass.: Lexington Heath, 1971); and Nathan Leites and Charles Wolf, Jr., *Rebellion and Authority: An Analytic Essay on Insurgent Conflicts* (Chicago: Markham, 1970).

General systems theory is not directly and clearly related to systems analysis, even though they share some fundamental assumptions. Nevertheless, general systems theory provides many elements for policy sciences. Let me, therefore, mention here some basic texts and collections, which well represent general systems theory: Kenneth F. Berrien, *General and Social Systems* (New Brunswick, N.J.: Rutgers University Press, 1968); Ludwig von Bertalanffy, *General Systems Theory: Foundations, Development, Applications* (New York: Braziller, 1968); Walter Buckley, ed., *Modern Systems Research for the Behavioral Scientist* (Chicago: Aldine, 1968); George J. Klir, *An Approach to General Systems Theory* (New York: Van Nostrand Reinhold, 1969) and E. J. Miller and A. K. Rice, *Systems of Organization: The Control of Task and Sentient Boundaries* (London: Tavistock, 1967).

A searching reexamination of some basic ideas of the systems approach and of systems analysis is C. West Churchman, *Challenge to Reason* (New York: McGraw-Hill, 1968). Very important and revealing is the experience of the Pentagon during the McNamara period with systems analysis, as discussed by two of the main actors, in the important book by Alain C. Enthoven and K. Wayne Smith, *How Much is Enough? Shaping the Defense Program, 1961–1969* (New York: Harper & Row, 1971). Also bringing out many real problems is Charles L. Schultze, *The Policies and Economics of Public Spending* (Washington, D.C.: The Brookings Institution, 1968). A very relevant case study is Frederick C. Mosher and John E. Harr, *Programming Systems and Foreign Affairs Leaderships: An Attempted Innovation* (New York: Oxford University Press, 1970).

Applied social sciences go through a period of heart-searching, as evidenced by the extensive literature dealing with their nature and functions. Especially interesting are the various committee reprints and reports, which dealt with applied social science issues in the United States, such as: The four volumes on *The Use of Social Research in Federal Domestic Programs,* A Staff Study for the Research and Technical Programs Subcommittee of the Committee on Government Operations, House of Representatives, April 1967 (Washington, D.C.: U.S. Government Printing Office, 1967); and the three volumes of hearings before the Subcommittee on Government Research of the Committee on Government Operations, United States Senate, on S. 836, *A Bill to Provide for the Establishment of the National Foundation for the Social Sciences*, February and June, 1967 (Washington, D.C.: U.S. Government Printing Office, 1967). Other illustrations include National Academy of Sciences, Advisory Committee on Government Programs in the Behavioral Sciences, National Research Council, *The Behavioral Sciences and the Federal Government* (Washington, D.C.: National Academy of Sciences, 1968); Special Commission on the Social Sciences of the National Sciences Board, *Knowledge Into Action: Improving the Nation's Use of the Social Sciences* (Washington: Superintendent of Documents, 1969); and Behavioral and Social Sciences Survey Committee under the auspices of the Committees on Problems and Policy, Social Sciences Research Council, *The Behavior and Social Sciences: Outlook and Needs* (Englewood Cliffs, N.J.: Prentice Hall, 1969). Similar interests in other countries are illustrated by the *Report of the Committee on Social Studies* (Chairman: Lord Heyworth, England, Cmnd. 2660, HMSO, 1965) and *The Social Sciences and the Policies of Government* (Paris: OECD, 1966).

Good relevant books and collections include Elizabeth T. Crawford and Albert D. Biderman, eds., *Social Scientists and International Affairs* (New York: John Wiley, 1969); Fred R. Harris, ed., *Social Science and National Policy* (Chicago: Aldine, 1970); and Irving L. Horowitz, ed., *The Uses and Abuses of Social Science* (New Brunswick, N.J.: Trans-Action Books, 1971). Very interesting and revealing is the historic treatment by Gene M. Lyons, *The Uneasy Partnership: Social Science and the Federal Government in the Twentieth Century* (New York: Russell Sage, 1969), which should be compared with studies of the relations between government and physical sciences, e.g., Michael D. Reagan, *Scence and the Federal Patron* (New York: Oxford University Press, 1969).

Nearly all of these books deal with the methods, orientations and functions of applied and nonapplied social sciences, rather than with substantive policy issues. The present inadequacies of social sciences as contributors to better illumination of policy issues—not to speak, their resolutions—is well brought out by many of the papers in Kermit Gordon, ed., *Agenda for the Nation* (Washington, D.C.: Brookings Institution, 1968). Nevertheless, some progress in a number of directions can be identified. These directions include, for instance, attempts in respect to social indicators, social experimentation, impact evalution and social innovation. Such attempts are respectively reflected in the following recent books: Eleanor Bernert Sheldon and Wilbert E. Moore, eds., *Indicators and Social Change: Concepts and Measurements* (New York: Russell Sage Foundation, 1968) and Bertram M. Gross, ed., *Social Intelligence for America's Future: Explorations in Societal Problems* (Boston, Mass.: Allyn & Bacon, 1969); George Fairweather,

Methods for Experimental Social Innovation (New York: John Wiley, 1968), and the very unusual book by Beatrice K. Rome and Sydney C. Rome, *Organizational Growth Through Decisionmaking: A Computer-Based Experiment in Educative Method* (New York: American Elsevier, 1971); Edward A. Suchman, *Evaluative Research: Principles and Practice in Public Service and Social Action Programs* (New York: Russell Sage Foundation, 1967); Harmon D. Stein, ed., *Social Theory and Social Invention* (Cleveland, Ohio: Press of Case Western Reserve University, 1968) and Victor A. Thompson, *Bureaucracy and Innovation* (Alabama: University of Alabama Press, 1969).

A different perspective from the point of view of actual attempts to utilize social sciences is provided in Walter Williams, *Social Policy Research and Analysis: The Experience in the Federal Social Agencies* (New York: American Elsevier, 1971). The absence of a social science meta-theory oriented towards policy-relevant theory building is well reflected in the excellent book by Robert Dubin, *Theory Building* (New York: Free Press, 1969).

In futures studies, it is necessary to distinguish between the growing flood of books dealing wth different possible or absurd futures and the steady but much slower development of an improved futures-studies methodology. Limiting myself to the latter, some of the better relevant books are: Erich Jantsch, *Technological Forecasting in Perspective* (Paris: OECD, 1967); James R. Bright, ed., *Technological Forecasting for Industry and Government: Methods and Applications* (Englewood Cliffs, N.J.: Prentice-Hall, 1968); William F. Butler and Robert A. Kavesh, eds., *How Business Economists Forecast* (Englewood Cliffs, N.J.: Prentice-Hall, 1966); Robert U. Ayres, *Technological Forecasting and Long-Range Planning* (New York: McGraw-Hill, 1969); and Francois Hetman, *The Language of Forecasting* (Paris: Futuribles, 1969). Also relevant is Michael Young, *Forecasting and the Social Sciences* (London: Heineman, 1968). Remarkable in the way it ties together futures perspectives and present policy-making needs in Donald N. Michael *The Unprepared Society: Planning for a Precarious Future* (New York: Basic Books, 1968). Two relevant new periodicals are *Futures* and *Technological Forecasting and Social Change*.

Policy Sciences relevant work proceeds in many additional directions. Those include, for instance, new models in political science, as illustrated by two books by R. L. Curry, Jr. and L. L. Wade, namely, *A Theory of Political Exchange* (Englewood Cliffs, N.J.: Prentice-Hall, 1968) and *A Logic of Public Policy: Aspects of Political Economy* (Belmont, Calif.: Wadsworth, 1970). Significant work also goes on in planning theory (and practice), as brought out in George A. Steiner, *Top Management Planning* (New York: Macmillan, 1969); and in two volumes by Alfred J. Kahn, namely *Theory and Practice of Social Planning and Studies in Social Policy and Planning* [both published by (New York: Russell Sage Foundation, 1969)]. Very important are also specific treatments of defined policymaking institutions and tools, such as David B. Bobrow and Judah L.

Schwartz, eds., *Computers and the Policy-Making Community: Applications to International Relations* (Englewood Cliffs, N.J.: Prentice-Hall, 1968); Sarane S. Boocock and E. O. Schild, eds., *Simulation Games in Learning* (Beverly Hills, Calif.: Sage, 1968); and Thomas E. Cronin and Sanford D. Greenberg, *The Presidential Advisory System* (New York: Harper & Row, 1969). More important in the longer range are attempts to develop broad systems models, such as Jay W. Forrester, *Urban Dynamics* (Cambridge, Mass.: M.I.T. Press, 1969). The latter book should be compared to two collections on urban problems which move on a different dimension, namely Daniel P. Mognihan, ed., *Toward A National Urban Policy* (New York: Basic Books, 1970) and Leo F. Schnore and Henry Fagin, ed., *Urban Research and Policy Planning*, Volume 1, Urban Affairs Annual Reviews (Beverly Hills, Calif.: Sage, 1967).

Keeping in mind the broad scope and extensive aims of policy sciences, relevant literature goes beyond any confined discipline and includes a variety of innovative contemplations. For instance, I regard the following books as definitely relevant to policy sciences, in the full sense of that term: David Hackett Fischer, *Historians' Fallacies: Toward a Logic of Historic Thought* (New York: Harper & Row, 1970); Albert O. Hirschman, *Exit, Voice, and Loyalty* (Cambridge, Mass.: Harvard University Press, 1970); Herbert A. Simon, *The Science of the Artificial* (Cambridge, Mass.: M.I.T. Press, 1969); and Charles T. Tart, ed., *Altered States of Consciousness* (New York: John Wiley, 1969).

To return the reader to reality and to remind him that policy sciences are directed towards making an impact on reality, let me conclude this subjectively selected list of recommended readings with Gerald Caiden, *Administrative Reform* (Chicago: Aldine, 1969).

Index

(Entries followed by n indicate information given in a footnote.)